A TEXT-BOOK OF
EXPERIMENTAL
PSYCHOLOGY

A TEXT-BOOK OF
EXPERIMENTAL PSYCHOLOGY

WITH LABORATORY EXERCISES

THIRD EDITION
PART II—LABORATORY EXERCISES
With 40 Figures and Diagrams

BY

CHARLES S. MYERS
M.A., M.D., Sc.D., F.R.S.,
FELLOW OF GONVILLE AND CAIUS COLLEGE,
CAMBRIDGE,
DIRECTOR OF THE NATIONAL INSTITUTE OF
INDUSTRIAL PSYCHOLOGY

AND

F. C. BARTLETT, M.A.
FELLOW OF ST JOHN'S COLLEGE,
UNIVERSITY READER IN EXPERIMENTAL PSYCHOLOGY,
DIRECTOR OF THE UNIVERSITY PSYCHOLOGICAL LABORATORY,
CAMBRIDGE

CAMBRIDGE
AT THE UNIVERSITY PRESS
1925

CAMBRIDGE
UNIVERSITY PRESS

University Printing House, Cambridge CB2 8BS, United Kingdom

Published in the United States of America by Cambridge University Press, New York

Cambridge University Press is part of the University of Cambridge.

It furthers the University's mission by disseminating knowledge in the pursuit of education, learning and research at the highest international levels of excellence.

www.cambridge.org
Information on this title: www.cambridge.org/9781107626027

© Cambridge University Press 1925

Second edition 1911
Reprinted 1922
First published 1925
Third edition 1925
First paperback edition 2013

A catalogue record for this publication is available from the British Library

ISBN 978-1-107-62602-7 Paperback

PREFACE TO THE THIRD EDITION

ALTHOUGH in this edition the greater part of the old matter has been incorporated, many new experiments have been introduced which are entirely due to Mr F. C. Bartlett. Some of these were devised by him while acting as Assistant to the Director of the University Psychological Laboratory at Cambridge; others were added when he succeeded me in the latter post. In this edition, therefore, his name fitly appears with mine on the title page. For the most part these new exercises concern the higher mental functions. They do not involve any special apparatus; they can be easily carried out; and they yield highly instructive results. They are indicative of the steady progress of experiment in psychology.

C. S. M.

LONDON,
August, 1925.

TABLE OF CONTENTS

	PAGE
Introductory	1
Free Association	4
Perception and Reproduction of Forms .	7
Recognition and Recall	11
Processes of Construction . . .	12
Processes of Analysis	14
Method of Mean Error	15
Limiting Method	16
Method of Serial Groups	18
Constant Method	19
Method of Equal Appearing Intervals .	20
Experiences of Identity and Difference .	23
Absolute Impression	23
Equal-Appearing Intervals of Brightness .	24
Reaction Times	26
Simple and Composite Reactions . .	35
Heat and Cold Spots	39
Colour Vision	41
Visual Acuity	47
Auditory Experience	48
Perception of Form and Size . . .	58
Perception of Distance and Movement .	60
Span of Attention	63
Imaging	66
Memory	69
Muscular and Mental Fatigue . . .	72
Mental Tests	76
Cutaneous and Thermal Sensations . .	77
Labyrinthine and Motor Sensations . .	80
Gustatory Sensations	85
Olfactory Sensations	87
Visual Sensations	88

	PAGE
Auditory Sensations	92
Olfactory Acuity	100
Sensory Adaptation	101
Tactual Localisation	103
Binocular Experience	105
Optical Illusions	108
Estimation of Time Intervals	110
Rhythm	110
The Memory Image	111
Muscular Practice	112
Fluctuations of Attention	113
Expression of Feeling	114
Statistical Methods	118

INTRODUCTORY.

An introductory course in experimental psychology serves two chief ends: it affords a training in the peculiar technique and methods of psychological experiment, and it illustrates the scope of experimental study in psychology. The actual results obtained from a class experiment, though they can hardly fail to be of interest, can but rarely be regarded as justifying sweeping conclusions. Accordingly from the beginning the student should concentrate his attention upon the methods which he is instructed to employ, and upon getting as clear a conception as possible of the nature and range of experiment in psychology. Frequently a careful and critical student, dissatisfied with his results, may be inclined to consider the experimental method unsuitable to the field of psychological investigation. It is certain that in no psychological test can the ideal experiment, in which all of the conditions are thoroughly under control, be performed. It is equally certain that we can never be quite sure that only one condition is being varied. But such facts do not affect the desirability that psychological observation and analysis should be carried out under conditions which have been rendered as definite as possible. It must from the outset be realised that as we can obtain only partial control and partial independent variation of conditions in psychological experiment, all experimental study must at present be supplemented by most careful attention to facts of general psychological observation and to results of general psychological analysis. The experimentalist in psychology must be a psychologist; otherwise the tendency will be towards the mere accumulation of numbers of facts which show very little coherence, and appear to lead nowhere in particular.

The present course is divided into four sections. The first three of these comprise thirty-two lessons and may be taken to represent a first year's work in experimental psychology. The first section is designed to give a training in the technique of psychological experiment, and is itself divided into two parts. The first six lessons deal with typical experiments the results of which require qualitative analysis, the second five with experiments treated by quantitative methods, while three lessons involving other special points of technique are added. In the second section a number of experiments directed to a study of the special senses are collected. It is assumed that certain of the commoner experiments on sensory processes will be demonstrated in lectures which accompany this course[1]. Accordingly the experiments which are to be performed in the practical class work, are those which by their nature are less suitable for general demonstration. But they must not be regarded as covering more than a part of the ground, and their results must be considered in conjunction with those of the demonstrations and with those of the additional experiments on sensory processes included in Section IV. In the third section a number of typical experiments on perception and the higher mental processes are collected. These again represent but a small selection from among the possible tests.

It is assumed that in general each student will work throughout the whole course in conjunction with a second student with whom he will act alternatively as experimenter and subject. The student who is going to act as experimenter will be expected to read beforehand the description of the experiments which he is to perform in any given practical class, and if necessary to prepare material for the experiment. An account of the course of each experiment, an analysis of the results, and the record of the subject's introspections must be written out as soon as the experiment in question has been completed, so that at the end of his course every student will have a complete note book of a practical class course in psychology, including the description of the experiments, the record of how they were conducted, the analysis of their results, and the introspective accounts of the experiences of the subject.

The general plan according to which each experiment will be written out by the student will be as follows:

1. General description of experiment.
2. Names of experimenter and subject.

[1] Some of these will be found included in Section IV.

3. Date and time of experiment, together with notes upon any remarks the subject may have to make about his mental condition at the time of the experiment, and notes upon any unusual feature of the external environment. The writing of these notes must be taken seriously. One of the main points of the course is to promote habits of psychological observation, and it is important from the beginning to get into the way of noting carefully everything that may appear to have any bearing upon the results.

4. Brief account of the course of the experiment, with particular reference to any modifications of the general procedure which may prove to be necessary.

5. The results of the experiment as observed by the experimenter.

6. The results of the experiment as observed by the subject expressed in terms of his own experience.

7. Summary of conclusions that may seem probable, and suggestions for improvement or development of the method of the experiment.

SECTION I.

The Technique of Psychological Experiment.

A. QUALITATIVE ANALYSIS OF EXPERIMENTAL RESULTS.

The first five lessons in the course are intended to provide practice for the subject in introspection, for the experimenter mainly in the giving of directions for experiment. The experiments should in general be carried out in three stages. First the experimenter will give to the subject his instructions. These must be made definite and unambiguous, and at the same time the aim of the experimenter will be to set the subject as completely at his ease as possible. In the subsequent experiment, the experimenter must keep a careful watch upon any specific influence of the instructions upon the results. One of the problems of this course for the experimenter is to determine in general the effect of "awareness of a task" upon experimental results.

In the second stage both experimenter and subject should concentrate their attention upon the actual performance of the task set.

In the third stage, the subject, either by dictation or writing, will give his introspective account of the course of the experiment. This will then be of the nature of immediate retrospection.

Occasionally attempt should be made to mingle stages two and three, so as to determine what are the main effects of the effort simultaneously to perform a task and to introspect its performance.

Experiment 1.

Free Association.

Materials required: Lists of words[1]; stop-watch; pen and paper.

[1] Any list of about 100 words prepared by the experimenter will serve the purposes of this experiment. Suitable printed lists may be obtained from practically any firm which supplies psychological apparatus.

The experimenter will obtain a list of words, and a stop-watch. The instructions to the subject are :

"I am going to read out to you a word. You are to listen and then to tell me the very first word that occurs to you after you have heard the word that I give you. Make no effort to get any particular kind of word, but give me at once any word that 'comes up,' as we say. I will give you five practice trials, and then we will begin the experiment proper."

The word pronounced by the experimenter is called the 'stimulus word,' that returned by the subject is called the 'reaction,' or 'response word.' The experimenter starts his stop-watch as he gives the stimulus word, and stops the watch as the subject gives the reaction word. The experimenter writes each reaction-word opposite its stimulus word, and records the time of the reaction.

When the list has been completed the subject should work carefully over the whole and try to say how he arrived at each reaction word, and in what form (*e.g.*, with or without visual imagery) each response occurred to him. The experimenter and the subject together should try to answer the question "How far are the associations really 'free'?" *i.e.*, is there not in every case some type (or types) of association to which a given subject is predisposed? Particularly note all the instances in which the time of the response as indicated by the stop watch is unusually prolonged. The subject should attempt to account for this delay. At the conclusion of the whole experiment the class should compare associations given by different subjects for the same list, and should discuss likenesses and differences. All the students should use these results to help them to answer the questions: "What is the significance for psychology of individual differences? How far do such differences render general conclusions in psychology hazardous?" At the conclusion of the experiment an attempt should be made to classify the associations given. A scheme of classification is suggested in Part I, p. 142. Attention should be paid to the relative frequencies of the different types of association.

Experiment 2.

CONSTRAINED ASSOCIATION.

Materials required: Lists of words[1]; stop-watch; pens and paper.

The experimenter will obtain from the demonstrator lists of words and a stop-watch.

(a) *Opposites test*.

The instructions to the subject are:

"I am going to read you a word. You are to listen, and then to tell me as quickly as possible the word whose significance you consider to be exactly opposite to that of the word given to you. You understand: you are to give me the word whose meaning is precisely the opposite to the meaning of the word which I shall give you. You will have three practice trials, and then the experiment proper will begin."

Results are to be recorded, analysed, and compared precisely as in the case of the 'free' association experiment.

(b) *Part-whole test*.

The instructions are:

"I am going to read you a word. You are to listen, and then to tell me as quickly as possible the name of the whole of which the given word names a part. You understand: I shall give you the name of a part of something, and you will give me the name of the whole of which it is a part. You will have three practice trials and then the experiment proper will begin."

Results are to be recorded, analysed and compared precisely as in the case of the 'free' association experiment.

(c) *Species-genus test*.

The instructions are:

"I am going to read you a word. You are to listen, and then to tell me the name of the genus of which the given word names a species. You understand: I shall give you the name of a species, and you will give me the name of the genus of which

---

[1] See note on p. 4.

it is a species. You will have three practice trials, and then the experiment proper will begin."

Results are to be recorded, analysed and compared precisely as in the case of the 'free' association experiment.

(d) Mixed relations test.

The list of words must be handed, face downwards, to the subject.

The instructions are:

"On this form are a number of words so arranged that three words appear on each line. The first two words on each line are related in a certain manner. You have to find a word related to the third word in the very same manner as the second is related to the first word, and to work in this way through the whole list, taking each line as you come to it. For example, you may see [write on paper for the subject to read]:

gold: yellow: blood:

and you would write for the fourth word *red*, since *red* is the colour of *blood* as *yellow* is the colour of *gold*. You will first be given three practice trials"—to be given on a separate form—"and then the experiment proper will begin."

Record the total time taken by the subject to deal with his form, analyse and compare results as in the case of the experiment on 'free' association.

Throughout the whole of these experiments the subject should make a special attempt to state how far and in what way he was aware of the relations involved.

At the conclusion of the experiment the class should attempt to formulate definitely the chief differences observed between 'free' and 'constrained' association.

Experiment 3.

PERCEPTION AND REPRODUCTION OF FORMS OF GROWING COMPLEXITY.

Materials required: Set of diagrams or forms of growing complexity of structure. If possible a tachistoscope for their exposure—but this is not essential. Pen and paper.

The experimenter must prepare beforehand a number of designs which he will arrange in groups according to their complexity of structure. The type of design and arrangement needed for this experiment may be illustrated as below; in regard to detail there may of course be variations from case to case. The designs are to be presented with momentary exposure, one at a time, starting with those of the simplest group, and proceeding to the more complex ones.

GROUP I. Simple designs and patterns not of necessity having any obvious significance, such as:

GROUP II. Designs containing somewhat more detail; some of them likely to suggest representations of concrete objects, and some more meaningless; such as:

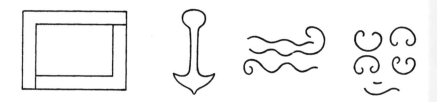

GROUP III. Designs which still form readily appreciable wholes, being built according to some appreciable plan, but containing yet more detail; such as:

GROUP IV. Designs which form a group by themselves, passing by simple addition of parts from a simple to a complicated form, such as:

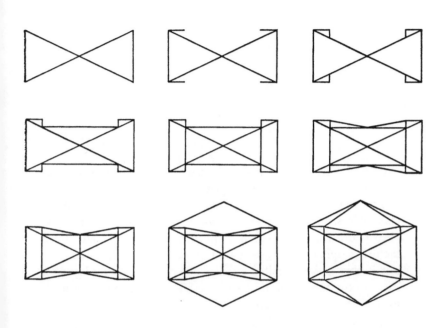

GROUP V. Fairly simple picture material of a concrete kind, of the type, for example, of:

or

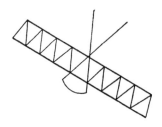

GROUP VI. Any complex picture material, such as illustrations from a newspaper or magazine.

The above types of material must all be prepared before the class meets, and should be of about ordinary postcard size, and clearly drawn. If possible, exposure should be made by a tachistoscopic method (see Part I, p. 322; this Part, pp. 64, 65); but if this is not possible exposure may be made by laying a card on the table with its face covered, and then uncovering it for a period of five seconds.

The instructions to the subject are:

"I am going to allow you to see a drawing or design for a very short period. I shall say 'Now' and then immediately uncover the drawing. Try to notice all of its details and, when I have covered up the design, to reproduce what you have seen."

The subject must attempt to report his *method* of observation in each case. This must be insisted upon, as the main purpose of the experiment at this stage is to provide practice in introspection directed upon the nature of perceptual process.

The further questions involved are: "What are the factors which enter into the perception of objects of the type here employed?"

"Is there any ground for believing that those factors increase in complexity as the objects themselves become structurally more complex?" (Consider, in reference to this question, what marks the psychologically 'simple.')

"Can the process of naming be shown to have any special influence upon processes of perceiving?"

"What light, if any, do experiments of this type throw upon the relation between perceiving and remembering?"

Experiment 4.
RECOGNITION AND RECALL.

Materials required: (*a*) All of the material employed in the last experiment, together with new material of the same type; (*b*) a set of twenty 'meaningless' curved patterns drawn in ink, ordinary postcard size; (*c*) a set of fifteen 'meaningless' forms cut out of thick cardboard, and of about half foolscap size.

[(*c*) will be provided.]

The experiment will proceed in the following stages:

Stage I. Present ten of the (*b*) set of designs. Spread them out on a table and allow any time up to but not exceeding 10 minutes for an examination of the whole set. The instructions are:

"I am going to place on the table a set of ten meaningless designs. I want you to notice as carefully as you can the details of the various designs so that you will know them should you meet with them again. You will be allowed plenty of time to make your observation, but should you be satisfied that you have completed your task before I call 'time', tell me, and I will remove the designs."

At the end of 10 minutes, or such time as the subject requires, mix up the ten designs with the others in the (*b*) set, and place the whole on one side out of sight of the subject.

Note the time at which the examination of the designs began.

Stage II. Ask the subject to recall as much as he is able of the material used in Experiment 3. The material recalled must be reproduced whenever possible, or described in detail.

Stage III. Ask the subject now to recall and reproduce the designs from the (*b*) set, which he saw in Stage I. Record time of recall.

Stage IV. Take five of the meaningless designs in the (*c*) set. Instruct subject: "I have here a number of forms cut out of cardboard. Close your eyes, and I will place your right forefinger on the starting-point of one of the forms. You will be able to trace the pattern of the form by feeling the cut edges of the cardboard. Trace the form slowly three times over. I will stop you when you come to the end of the pattern, and then place your finger on the starting point again. Do not open your eyes until I give you permission." Remove the cardboard before allowing the subject to open his eyes. Repeat procedure with all five patterns. The patterns should be marked so that the experimenter can replace them in exactly the same position in relation to the observer in Stage VII of the experiment.

Stage V. Give to the subject the whole of the old and new material in the (*a*) set. Instruct him thus: "Choose from these all the designs or pictures which you have seen before."

Stage VI. Give to the subject the whole of the material in set (*b*). Instruct him to "Choose from these all the patterns which you have seen before."

Stage VII. Ask the subject to attempt to recall the motor patterns made by tracing over the cut-out forms. Then give the subject the whole fifteen to trace with his right forefinger, as before, making sure that they are the same way up as before, and ask him to select those which he recognises.

At each stage the subject will concentrate his attention upon the processes and methods of recall, and upon the apparent mechanism of recognition.

The experimenter and subject should discuss any differences that may appear between the amount recalled and the amount recognised.

Experiment 5.

PROCESSES OF CONSTRUCTION.

1. *Materials required*: Pen and paper.

The experimenter must prepare his material beforehand. Taking ten sheets of square 'scribbling' paper, he should subdivide each sheet into a number of parallelograms as explained below. He might for example have:

or or

and so on. Five of these sheets are to be cut along the lines of division and the pieces placed in separate envelopes. The other five are not to be cut, but the isolated pieces are to be drawn to scale on a sheet of paper, and placed in any position. Thus:

Take a second ten sheets, making this time angular divisions, as:

cut five and draw five, as with the parallelograms.

In the experiment (*a*) for the cut pieces: take all the pieces from a particular envelope and place them before the subject, putting them on a table in any positions, Say: "Here are a number of pieces of paper. Fitted together they will form a square. Make the square by putting the pieces into their proper place." Continue for the five squares.

The experimenter must note carefully the subject's method of work, and the subject must introspect his effort of construction after the completion of each square.

(*b*) For the pieces drawn, place any paper with the drawings of the separate pieces before the subject. Say: "On this paper are drawn separately a number of shapes which, when they are put together, can be formed into a square. Here is a piece of 'scribbling' paper. Suppose it to be the completed square. Draw on it how the pieces would need to be fitted together so as to form the square." Continue for the five squares.

Subject's introspections are obtained as before. Special consideration should be given to the differences which actual manipulation, occurring in the case of the cut pieces, and wanting in that of the drawn pieces, may make.

2. *Materials required*: Some simple mechanical appliance which has been taken to pieces. This must be obtained by the experimenter. Admirable material is provided by simple forms of lock and key such as may be obtained from any ironmonger for a few pence.

Instructions: "Here are the parts of a simple mechanical appliance. Put them together so that the whole will work." Introspections must be obtained as before.

3. *Materials required*: Pen and paper.

The experimenter must prepare for this beforehand. He will take a short paragraph of ordinary English prose of from ten to twenty words and rewrite it, changing the order of words and sentences in such a way that the meaning is at first sight obscured. This he will place before the subject. His instructions will be: "Here is a piece of English prose the order of the words of which has been changed. Reconstruct it, so that it makes sense." Introspections must be obtained as before. The purpose of the experiment is mainly to give practice in introspection directed upon the processes of mental construction.

Experiment 6.

PROCESSES OF ANALYSIS.

The material for these experiments must be prepared beforehand by the experimenter.

1. The experimenter must select two passages of prose containing ideas which can be expressed in a sentence or two. In the experiment he will read these once to the subject. The instructions are: "I am going to read you a passage of English prose. Listen carefully, and then tell me in as brief a form as you can what you consider to be the essential ideas of the passage."

The subject will give his introspections as soon as he has completed his analysis of a given passage.

2. The experimenter draws a number (say ten) of fairly complicated designs, which must differ from one another as much as possible, save that they *all* contain *one* common feature, and certain of them contain an additional feature common only to these. Place these ten designs *one after the other* before the subject. The instructions are:

"Look at these designs and see if you can discover any feature or features common to more than two of them."

The subject must give as precise an account as possible of his procedure.

3. (*a*) A simple piece of mechanism must be obtained by the experimenter who will direct the subject to take it to pieces and determine the working relations of the parts. As before, some simple form of lock and key is a useful type of material.

(*b*) A second piece of mechanism will be provided, and the experimenter will instruct the subject to determine the working relations of the parts without taking the model to pieces.

Throughout the whole of these experiments the subject must take particular pains to keep a close introspective record.

B. EXPERIMENTS INVOLVING THE USE OF THE PSYCHO-PHYSICAL METHODS.

If the previous experiments have been properly carried out, the student will have had considerable practice in the observation of a variety of mental processes. He will further have realised very definitely the need for as strict a technique as possible if the results of psychological experiment are to yield precise conclusions. In the second part of this section, therefore, the emphasis will be predominantly upon *methods*. The work in itself is apt to appear dull. But its importance can hardly be overestimated, and the student should apply himself to see that all the demands are strictly observed. The whole of the work of this part should be prefaced by a most careful reading of Part I, chapters XV and X, and continual reference to these chapters should be made throughout the experiments. Whenever any apparatus is provided for the use of the student, his description of the course of the experiments should contain an explanatory diagram of the apparatus used.

Experiment 7.

THE METHOD OF MEAN ERROR.

For a description of the method and of the manipulation of the experimental results, see Part I, pp. 189–92.

The experimenter should apply this method to an investigation of the conditions affecting the accuracy with which the subject can make one line equal to another. An inexpensive form of apparatus for class work is one in which two white threads are displayed upon a black screen, the length of either being adjustable by an arrangement which the subject can easily manipulate behind the screen. A series of ten observations should be taken under each of the following conditions: the standard lying (*a*) to the right of, (*b*) to the left of, the variable; and a further series should be taken to show any differences dependent on whether the subject has to shorten or lengthen the variable line in order to make it equal to the standard. The apparatus should be held so that the plane of the screen cuts the line of vision at right angles; that is to say, it should be held vertically in front of, or horizontally immediately below, the eyes.

A few preliminary practice experiments should precede the actual record of results. Every group of ten observations should be divided into two sub-groups, each of five observations, and the order of taking the various sub-groups should be so arranged that the influences of practice and fatigue may be nearly constant for each group. Within the limited time available in class work, the complete equalisation of conditions is, of course, impossible.

The experimenter determines the constant and average error and the mean variable error (*a*) from the whole of the results obtained, and also from the results obtained when the variable lies (*b*) to the left and (*c*) to the right of the standard line. He may thence deduce the space error. He should also determine the constant error according as the variable has been (*d*) shortened or (*e*) lengthened by the subject.

Experiment 8.

The Limiting Method.

For a description of this method and of how the results of experiments should be dealt with, read carefully Part I, pp. 192–6. The method is here to be used to investigate the size-weight illusion.

The experimenter employs the series of canisters (fig. 1) provided in the laboratory, one of them being half the breadth or half the height of the others. This, loaded with shot so as to weigh, say, 200 grams, serves as the standard, while the larger canisters, differently weighted, serve as the variables. A metronome or silently swinging pendulum may be used to mark the rate with which the subject must raise and lower each canister, and to preserve a constant interval between handling each member of the various pairs of canisters. A horizontal cord should be stretched, say, six inches, above the height of the canister so as to ensure a constant height of lift. The series of canisters is screened by the experimenter from the subject's view. The experimenter successively places the canisters so that the subject lifts each canister from the same spot; sometimes the standard, sometimes the variable, is lifted first. In this way the space and time errors (Part I, pp. 191, 192) are avoidable. The subject grasps each canister by the body, not by the handle.

FIG. 1. The small canister is employed with the larger ones in measuring the 'size-weight' illusion. Only two of the larger canisters are here figured; in actual experiment a considerably larger number is necessary. The larger canisters are to external appearance exactly similar, but they are differently weighted with shot, the lids being removable. The canisters are *usually* lifted by one finger which is inserted beneath the handle.

The experimenter first plans a series of pairs of lifts by the limiting method in order roughly to determine the variable weight which appears to the subject equal to the standard. In these preliminary experiments the variables should range between 250 and 400 grams, and differ by increments of 50 grams. The series should be regularly lifted in ascending and descending order.

Then a series of experiments may be conducted in which the variable canisters differ by increments of 10 grams, and the value of the central variable is that which (as determined in the preliminary experiment) appears approximately equal to the smaller canister, *i.e.* the standard. At least five variables should be used, and each should be presented with the standard, the limiting method being used.

The subject's answers, 'heavier,' 'equal,' 'doubtful,' or 'lighter,' should uniformly refer to the second canister lifted. The experimenter divides the 'equal' and 'doubtful' answers equally between the 'heavier, and 'lighter' answers (Part I, p. 201). He determines (by one of the methods alluded to in Part I, pp. 198, 199) the value of a (hypothetical) canister which would give equal numbers of 'heavier' and 'lighter' answers. This is evidently the weight of the variable which appears to be equal to that of the standard. We have thus measured the size-weight illusion.

Experiment 9.

THE METHOD OF SERIAL GROUPS.

For a description of this modification of the Limiting Method see Part I, pp. 196-7. The method is here to be used to investigate the Spatial Threshold. Record and attempt analysis of the results of 'catch' experiments.

The subject rests his arm comfortably on the table, extensor surface downwards. The experimenter marks in ink a point on the subject's forearm, which is to indicate the middle of the region to be investigated. Having found a distance which is just sufficient to be decidedly above the subject's spatial threshold, the experimenter applies the compass points, thus separated, to the subject's arm for about two seconds. The latter, having his eyes closed, decides whether he is being touched by two points or by one. The compass should be applied ten times with both points touching, and ten times with a single point touching the skin, in irregular order. Then the distance between the points is to be reduced by five millimetres, and another series of twenty stimulations is begun. The distance is in this way reduced, until two wrong answers in ten are obtained for the answers to double touches. This may be conventionally regarded as the threshold.

Care must be taken to apply the two points simultaneously, and with equal and constant pressure. When one point is used, it should be applied near one or other of the spots to which the two points are applied.

The subject should carefully note his experiences and take care that they are recorded. Sensations of cold should be avoided. The subject should, in particular, analyse his experiences near the threshold. A second series of experiments should be made so that he may discover, so far as possible, the basis of his improvement with practice. A third series may be made, in which the subject is told each time by the experimenter whether his answer is correct or not. Here he should try to find the reasons for his wrong answers, and the experimenter should note the results of this modification of the experiment.

It is worth while to bear in mind the proposal which has been put forward by Binet, that subjects are divisible into three classes, according to their behaviour in this experiment. The *simplistes* only record a double touch as such, when two distinct tactual sensations are present. They show an abrupt transition from answers which are all correct, to answers many of which are wrong. They never err in describing a single touch as double. The *interprétateurs* make ample use of inference, and avail themselves of the difference between the effects produced by double stimulation and those produced by single stimulation, even when a double touch is not actually experienced (Part I, p. 219). Their threshold is less definite. The *distraits* are those who, owing to their liability to distraction, are apt to confuse the difference between single and double touches, and thus sometimes describe single as double touches. This latter illusion, however, is certainly not always due merely to lack of attention; its causation requires future investigation.

Experiment 10.

THE CONSTANT METHOD.

For a description of the Constant Method see Part I, pp. 197–202. The method is here to be used for the investigation of the size-weight illusion. (See Experiment 8.)

Compare the results now obtained with those secured when the Limiting Method was used.

Experiment 11.

THE METHOD OF EQUAL APPEARING INTERVALS.

For a description of the method of equal appearing intervals see Part I, p. 202. Note particularly that "there is no single method of equal appearing intervals. It is merely a special instance of the application of the method of mean error, the limiting method, or the constant method to a particular problem."

Two experiments are to be attempted:

(1) Arrange three pairs of weights, *a–f,* so that the difference between *a* and *b* appears equal to the difference between *c* and *d,* which again appears equal to the difference between *e* and *f.* When this has been done compare the difference between *e* and *f* with that between *a* and *b.* Should these differences *not* appear equal, consider the probable explanation. Obtain introspection throughout.

(2) The student should familiarise himself with the apparatus devised for recording equal intervals of time on the smoked surface of a revolving drum. An electrically vibrating tuning-fork may be connected in the same circuit with a time marker (fig. 2). But it is more convenient to use a specially devised clock (fig. 2), bearing a lever which records fifths of seconds or whole seconds, as desired.

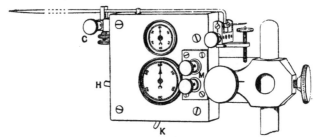

FIG. 2. Clock Time Marker.

The upper of the two dials records minutes, the lower seconds. The clock is started and stopped by the lever *H.* Movement of the lever *K* restores the clock hands to starting-point (60). The clock is wound by turning a nut on the side opposite to that shown in the figure. On the same side is a small stud which changes the rate of movement of the recording lever. This can be made to rise and fall every second or every fifth of a second. Its excursions may be recorded directly on a travelling smoked surface, or they may be used to interrupt either of two electric circuits, the terminals for which are shown at *M.*

The recording apparatus should, even for class purposes, be set up in a different room from that in which the subject sits whose accuracy of time estimation is under investigation. The most reliable method of presenting to the subject any desired interval of time is attained by the use of a uniformly rotating metal arm which during rotation comes into contact with two (or more) sets of terminals; the result of such contacts being to close (or to open) electric circuits, and thereby to produce two or more (*e.g.* telephonic) sounds absolutely alike in character and separated by an interval dependent on the

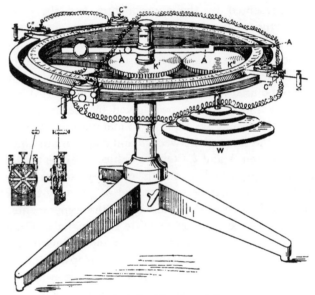

FIG. 3. The Leipzic 'Time Sense' Apparatus.

The arm A is driven by the cog wheels K', K'', and these by the wheel W, whic is connected with a reliable (clockwork or other form of) motor. As it revolves, the arm touches a number of contacts, C', C'', C''', C^{iv}. A contact, drawn from two aspects, is separately shown in a corner of the figure.

rate of rotation of the metal arm, and the distance between any two sets of the metal terminals, which can be accurately varied at will.

In place of this apparatus (fig. 3) the interval may be presented to the subject by two auditory signals, given from the room in which the recording apparatus stands, and transmitted to the subject by means of a telephone 'buzzer.' Or still more simply, a second individual sitting not too near the subject, with a watch in hand, may give the two stimuli by tapping twice on a Morse key, and the time estimation is made by the subject tapping similarly on a second key.

If Morse keys are used, they should be so arranged that the taps, made on each, are communicated to a single time signal which is brought to write on the recording surface of the drum directly above the movements of the lever of the time marker. By this arrangement, both the length of the interval presented by the experimenter and the estimated interval returned by the subject can be measured, and compared. The experimenter must be careful to mark each of the experimenter's intervals on the drum, so that later he can always distinguish them from the subject's intervals. The two keys may be used in a variety of ways. The interval between two taps, *a* and *b*, having been given by the experimenter's key, the subject may be required to make a third tap *c* on his key, when the interval between *b* and *c* appears to him equal to that between *a* and *b*. Or the subject may be required to make two taps, *c* and *d*, on his own key, separated by an interval equal to that between *a* and *b*, given by the experimenter. In this case, the intervals of the experimenter and subject may be recorded on separate time signals. Or, again, the experimenter, after having given *a* and *b*, himself gives the tap *c* after a definite fixed interval has elapsed, the subject being enjoined to give the fourth tap *d* on his own key when the intervals between *c* and *d* and between *a* and *b* appear to him equal.

By one of these methods, a series of experiments should be made for intervals of different lengths; five tests, for example, being made for intervals lying between 10 and 12 seconds, five for intervals between 5 and 6 seconds, five for intervals of about 4 seconds, five for 3, and so on for 2, $1\frac{1}{2}$, 1, $\frac{1}{2}$ and $\frac{1}{4}$ seconds. The sounds should be given with uniform loudness, and between each group of five tests the subject should carefully record the results of introspective analysis. When the interval is very small, the experimenter will himself be unable to present it exactly, but this is of little moment as the interval which he presents will be accurately measurable on the drum to which his taps are transmitted.

The percentage error, positive or negative, should be calculated for each estimation, and the nature and extent of the error for the different lengths of intervals, together with the position of the indifference point, should be investigated. The results may be further treated in their original groups of five, with the object of testing the variability of the error for different lengths of interval; but for reliable results a greater number of data must be obtained, and the order in which they are obtained must be taken into consideration.

Using the apparatus consisting of the Morse keys, telephone buzzer and time signals, determine a time interval *a–b*, which appears exactly half the length of a given time interval *a–c*. Employ one of the fundamental methods which has not been used in (1).

Experiment 12.

EXPERIENCES OF IDENTITY AND DIFFERENCE.

Read first the whole of chapter XIX, Part I. Attempt to illustrate the application of Weber's Law by an experiment with weights, using the limiting method described in Part I, p. 192. Carry out the experiment with great care, and endeavour to obtain introspections at intervals throughout the series of tests.

Experiment 13.

THE ABSOLUTE IMPRESSION.

First read pp. 256–260, Part I.

The experiment here described should be performed. A standard weight, *S*, of 400 grams, and four variable weights, $S \pm d$, and $S \pm 2d$, may be used, *d* being 20 grams. The answers should be scheduled as follows:

Order	$S-2d$	$S-d$	$S+d$	$S+2d$
1				
2				
3				
4				

Here the percentage of correct judgments, when S is lifted with $S-2d$ and $S-d$, corresponds to the a judgments, and the percentage of correct judgments, when S is lifted with $S+d$ and $S+2d$, corresponds to the b judgments of the text. The four orders in the schedule refer to the possible combinations of different temporal and spatial orders (e.g. a_1, a_2, a_3, a_4) mentioned in the text.

The variables should be used with the standard in quite haphazard order, until (say) each variable has been presented five times in each of the four orders, that is until 80 judgments have been recorded. 'Doubtful' and 'equal' judgments may be divided equally between the right and wrong judgments (Part I, p. 201).

Eighty answers will provide material for the student to elucidate the influence of the absolute impression, the general tendency of judgment and the effects of time and space order. But no confidence can be placed in the results of so few observations.

Experiment 14.

EQUAL-APPEARING INTERVALS OF BRIGHTNESS.

Two 'standard' grey papers, a and b, of different brightnesses, are presented upon a black or white ground. Accompanying them is a third paper, the variable c, one of a series of various greys. By one of the recognised psycho-physical methods the experimenter has to find a paper c of such brightness that to the subject the difference between a and b appears equal to that between b and c. The papers must be of exactly the same size and uniformly illuminated. The light values of the various grey papers having been determined as described below, the relation of the intensities of the stimuli a, b, c to the sensation differences can be investigated. The chief causes of departure from Weber's law have been already sufficiently discussed in the text.

The light values of the grey papers may be determined in the following manner. It may be assumed that the greatest value of reflected light obtainable from the surface of a paper is afforded by a sheet of baryta-covered paper. This will serve as the standard, and will be given the value of 360. The light values of other white, grey, and black papers may be expressed in terms of the standard, a paper yielding half the light of the standard receiving the value 180 and so on. It may be further assumed that an absolutely black back-ground is obtainable by looking into a long tube, say 75 cm. long and about 30 cm. in diameter, closed save for a small opening, and lined with black velvet. Before this opening a colour wheel is set up, and on the colour wheel is rotated a smaller disc of the paper to be tested and a projecting sector of larger radius, of the standard paper. This sector being rotated with sufficient speed before the black aperture, flicker is finally abolished, and an outer ring is obtained which is comparable with the smaller disc on the colour wheel. The arc of the sector is increased or diminished until the two colourless surfaces are identical. The light value of the paper to be tested is then given by the number of degrees covered by the arc. Of course, any white paper may be used as, and in place of, the standard, if it has previously been standardised with the latter.

The most convenient manner of arranging the papers on the colour wheel is here indicated (fig. 4). A represents the diameter of the smaller disc, the paper to be tested. B represents on the same scale the standard paper which is placed behind A on the colour wheel. The size of the projecting

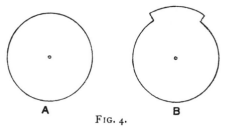

A   FIG. 4.   B

sector is so chosen that on rotation of the wheel the outer ring is darker than the inner disc. Behind B is placed a second piece of the standard paper B' precisely similar to it. Then B

and B' can be accurately super-imposed, or B' can be turned round so that more of its segment comes to project beyond the segment of B, until upon rotation of the wheel the desired match is obtained.

When once the light value of a second paper has been estimated, the value of any third paper may be readily found without the use of a dark chamber by rotating a disc of the latter paper on the colour wheel, while behind it are arranged two larger discs of the already standardised papers, slit from centre to periphery in the ordinary fashion, and movable one over the other, until on rotation the outer ring and inner disc match one another. If, for example, the match requires $125°$ of the standard paper and $235°$ of the already standardised grey paper, and if their light values be 360 and 75 respectively, then the light value of the paper in the inner ring is

$$125 + \frac{235 \times 75}{360} = 173\cdot96 \text{ nearly.}$$

Experiment 15.

REACTION TIMES.

Reaction-time tests are needed in connexion with a considerable number of psychological experiments. They have their own technique, which must be thoroughly learned, and also the apparatus employed must be well understood. Experiment 15 will be a class demonstration on the apparatus and method of the reaction time experiment. Diagrams should be made by the student of the setting of all the apparatus demonstrated. He must not be satisfied until he is able readily to set up and to explain the different types of reaction-time apparatus which are available.

Reaction times are most conveniently and accurately determined by interruptions in an electric circuit; a current being 'made' (or 'broken') at the moment of exhibition of the stimulus, and being 'broken' (or 'made') by the response of the subject.

The response usually consists in lifting the finger from a Morse telegraphic key, or it may consist in lip movement or in vocalisation. For the two last modes of response a lip key or a voice key is used, in which the electric current is broken by movements of the lip or by movements of a membrane thrown into vibration by the voice.

The appliances by which the current may be made (or broken) at the moment of exhibition of the stimulus are of various kinds, depending on the nature of the stimulus. The simplest available apparatus is a Morse key, which, when sharply and suddenly pressed upon, serves to give a sound stimulus and at the same time closes (or breaks) the electric circuit. But for greater convenience, and to insure uniformity of stimulus, the sound hammer (fig. 5) is preferable. In this

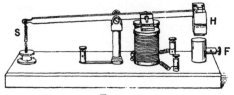

FIG. 5.

instrument a steel hammer, H, strikes against a steel foot, F, being drawn to the latter by means of an electro-magnet against the resistance of a spiral spring, S.

For visual reactions various forms of apparatus exist, involving movement of a shutter or a pendulum, and so designed that a current is made or broken at the moment of exhibition of the stimulus. It is essential that the visual stimulus should

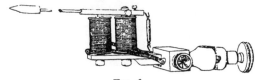

FIG. 6.

be presented silently, and in muscular reactions that the stimulus be exposed immediately the screen begins to move. Otherwise the subject is apt to react to a noise or to the initial movement of the screen, instead of to the desired visual stimulus.

Reaction times may be recorded by the graphic method; a time signal (fig. 6) and a time marker (fig. 7) being brought to bear, one above the other, upon a travelling smoked surface. The time signal is arranged in the same electric circuit with

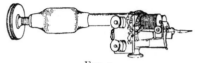

the two pieces of apparatus above described, which present the stimulus and receive the reagent's response, respectively. The time marker

FIG. 7.

records the vibrations of an electrically driven tuning-fork, vibrating, say, 50 or 100 times per second. By this means a tracing like the following may be obtained:

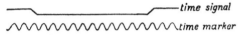

Hipp's chronoscope[1], however, is a far more convenient instrument for recording reaction times (figs. 8, 9, 10). The

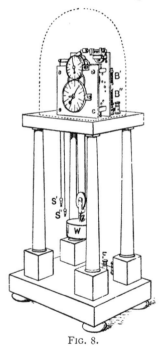

FIG. 8.

clockwork of the chronoscope is started by pulling on one of the two hanging cords, S', S'' (fig. 9), and it is stopped by pulling on the other cord. It is driven by a weight, W, which is raised by a key fitting into the centre of the lower dial. The crown wheels, C' and C'' (fig. 9), which lie near the front of the clock, have 100 teeth. The balance wheel, E, lying above and behind the crown wheels, is regulated by a small tongue of steel, T, which is thrown into movement by the starting of the clock, and is accurately tuned to vibrate 1000 times per second. This steel tongue thus allows a single tooth of the balance wheel to escape every thousandth part of a second. The two dials, D', D'', are divided into hundredth

<hr />

[1] This instrument is undoubtedly of English origin, having been first made in 1840 by Wheatstone. A specimen was seen by Hipp at Karlsruhe in 1842, who subsequently constructed the model which goes by his name.

parts. The hand of the upper dial revolves therefore ten times every second, and each division of the dial corresponds to a thousandth part of a second, *i.e.* to 1^{σ}. The hand of the lower dial is geared so as to revolve once every 10 seconds, each division of this dial corresponding to one-tenth of a second, *i.e.* to 100^{σ}.

While the clockwork of the chronoscope continues in action, the hands of the dials may be arrested or started at any moment

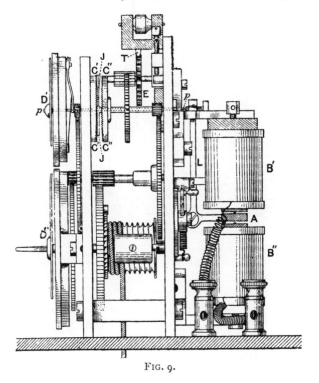

FIG. 9.

by means of the electro-magnetic mechanism at the rear of the instrument. For this purpose, either the upper or the lower pair of bobbins, B', B'' (in rare cases both pairs) may be used at will; the lower or upper spiral springs, S', S'' (fig. 10), being made appropriately tense by adjustment of the controlling levers, H', H'', which are placed at the sides of the instrument. By this arrangement, after the current has ceased to flow through those bobbins which are being used, the armature, *A*, is immediately released from contact with the bobbins.

The movement of the armature, thus brought about by one or other pair of bobbins, serves to vary the play of the vertical rod, *L*, connected with the armature, *A*, upon the upper axis or spindle, *p p*, which passes horizontally from the upper dial through the hollow axis of the crown wheels, *C'* and *C''*, to the back of the instrument. When the armature is pulled down (by the action of the lower springs or magnets), the spindle, *p p*, and the hand of the upper dial are drawn back, so that a small cross-bar, *J J*, fixed on the spindle, fits into one of the teeth of the hinder crown wheel, *C''*, through which the spindle passes. The movements of this crown wheel are thus communicated to the spindle and to the hands of the dials. When, on the other hand, as in fig. 9, the armature is held up (by the action of the upper springs or magnets), the cross-bar, *J J*, of the upper spindle no longer remains in the teeth of the crown wheel, *C''*; the spindle and the hands are seen to come forward, so that the cross-bar of the former now engages in the other crown wheel, *C'*, placed slightly nearer the front of the clock, which only differs from the former in that it is fixed instead of being movable.

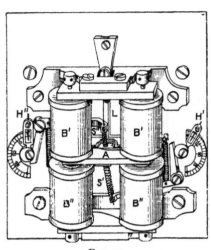

FIG. 10.

Thus, in the former position of the spindle the hands move, while in the latter they are thrown out of action, although the clockwork is continuously in movement; and as these two positions are determined by the closure or interruption of an electric current, we are enabled, by putting the terminals, *F*, of the chronoscope in the same circuit with the rest of the reacting apparatus, to record the length of time in which the dial hands have revolved between the exhibition of the stimulus and the response of the reagent. Thus if A (fig. 11) be the sound hammer, B the battery or other source of the current,

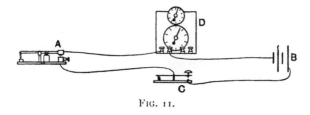

FIG. 11.

C the subject's key, and D be one of the two pairs of terminals of the chronoscope; then, when the key is depressed, the circuit will be closed when the stimulus is exhibited (*i.e.* when the sound hammer falls), and will be broken when the subject reacts. With this arrangement, those two terminals of the chronoscope must be chosen which allow of magnetisation of the lower pair of bobbins. If now the clockwork of the chronoscope be started, movement of the clock hands is effected by making, and is arrested by breaking, the circuit. Supposing that, before such a reaction experiment, the hands of the lower and upper dials be at 35 and 80 respectively, the experimenter records their position as 3580. If after the reaction they occupy the respective positions of 37 and 42, he subtracts 3580 from 3742, and obtains the reaction time 162 in terms of σ.

[This is the simplest arrangement of the chronoscope; in which the act of exhibiting the stimulus and the response of the subject respectively make and break the chronoscope current. It is, however, sometimes desirable that the act of exhibiting the stimulus should break the chronoscope current instead of making the current, in which case the upper instead of the lower bobbins of the chronoscope must be employed; so that when the current is broken the hands of the dials are instantly put into action, and when it is re-made by the subject they are again put out of action. In this case the subject reacts by closing the current. But for accurate work it is undesirable that the response of the subject should consist in making a contact (a slightly variable error being necessarily introduced by such procedure). This may be avoided if the battery current, B (fig. 12), be given the choice of passing through (i) a circuit

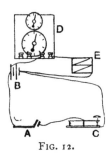

FIG. 12.

of raised resistance containing the upper bobbins of the chronoscope, D, or through (ii) an alternate circuit of lower resistance in which are placed the exhibiting apparatus, A, and the reacting apparatus, C. The resistance in (i) is raised by the use of a rheocord, E. In this arrangement the current flows through the higher resistance circuit, *i.e.* through the chronoscope, until the stimulus is exhibited; whereupon the lower resistance circuit is completed and the current in the chronoscope circuit is so far reduced that the magnets of the chronoscope no longer restrain the hands from moving. As soon as the subject reacts, the lower resistance circuit is again broken, so that the current must needs confine itself to the chronoscope circuit and thus arrests the movement of the hands.]

The chronoscope requires careful treatment in order to insure uniformity and accuracy of readings. A commutator must always be introduced into the chronoscope circuit, so that the direction of the current may be reversed after each individual reaction, thereby preventing permanent magnetisation of the soft iron core within the bobbins. The intensity of the current should be of a known and constant value. For this purpose a rheocord and a galvanometer (or ammeter) are employed. The springs of the chronoscope must be safeguarded from fatigue.

The reliability of the chronoscope must be tested by some form of control instrument. One of the best-known forms, the control hammer (fig. 13), essentially consists of a hammer, H, which during its fall successively makes and breaks (or breaks and re-makes), at L', L'', a current flowing through the chronoscope. The actual time occupied in the fall of the hammer may be afterwards determined by attaching a piece of smoked paper to the hammer and by recording on it the vibrations of a stationary tuning-fork. The control time may be altered by varying the position of the weighted counterpoise or by lowering or raising the electro-magnet, *B*, through which an independent current passes, holding up the hammer until the time has come for its release.

[So long as alternate circuits (as shown, for example, in fig. 12) are not employed in the reaction current, the error of the chronoscope, as tested by the control instrument, is usually the same for longer as for shorter intervals of time. When the error is proportionate to the length of the interval, we may

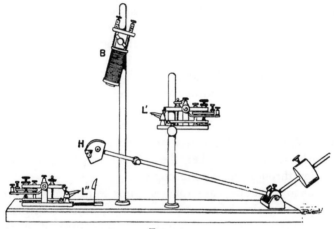

FIG. 13.

suspect that the clockwork runs faultily, the error lying perhaps in the teeth or in the escapement.

Assuming, however, that the clockwork of the laboratory instrument is not at fault, we turn our attention to another source of error. A latent period of time necessarily elapses between the closure of the current and the attraction of the armature. Another latent period elapses between the breaking of the current and the release of the armature. It is desirable that these two intervals should be equal. They are each due, in part, to mechanical inertia, to which is added the gradual growth of magnetism in the case of the former, and remanent magnetism in the case of the latter period. That is to say, magnetisation does not at once reach its full height, nor does it abruptly cease.

These two intervals may, in certain cases, be of considerable length, relatively to the time of running of the clockwork. They are affected by changing either the tension of the springs or the intensity of the current. It is found convenient in practice to vary only the current intensity.

Let us suppose that the hands are running when the chronoscope current is closed. According as the time recorded by the chronoscope exceeds or falls short of the value of the true control time, the flow of current should be diminished or increased by increasing or decreasing the resistance of a rheocord placed in the chronoscope circuit. The mean variation of the error may be often reduced by regulating the tension of the springs against which the armature of the chronoscope works.]

The chronoscope should be controlled before, and at the end of, every series, and in the middle of a prolonged series of reactions. The mean variation of a series of control tests should not exceed one-hundredth of the mean of the recorded times. After each individual test the commutator must be regularly reversed, so that the current is passed in either direction through the chronoscope.

Erroneous readings are apt from time to time to arise from improper vibration of the steel tongue, T, which controls the balance wheel, E, of the chronoscope. Sometimes it vibrates with half its proper frequency, sometimes it shows other forms of irregularity. After a little experience, however, the proper pitch of the tone, which the tongue should emit before a control time or reaction time is taken, is easily recognised.

Care must be taken to interpret the position of the more slowly moving index of the chronoscope dials in the light of information yielded by the other index. Supposing, for example, that the former points exactly to 35 and that the latter points to 98, the reading must be taken as 3498, not as 3598. Were the latter the real reading, the index would point nearly to 36, instead of pointing to 35.

The experimenter and the subject are now in a position to take a series of ten control times with the control hammer,—

using the upper or the lower electro-magnets of the chrono-scope, whichever are required for the ensuing reaction experiments.

Experiment 16.

SIMPLE AND COMPOSITE REACTIONS.

These experiments afford an excellent opportunity for the student to gain practice in the application of statistical methods to experimental results and in this connexion the examples recorded on pp. 118–121 should be studied. Apply similar statistical treatment to the reaction times obtained in the present experiments.

(*a*) *Simple reactions:*

The subject should, if possible, be seated in a quiet room, remote from that in which the chronoscope is placed. An assistant should be with him, in order to record observations of the latter's behaviour during reaction (*e.g.* premature reactions) and to take down from him any introspective notes. The room in which the subject sits contains the apparatus exhibiting the stimulus, the key by which he responds to it, and an electric signal of some kind whereby the experimenter is able to warn the subject to prepare himself for the reaction. When this signal sounds, the subject gets ready, and if a finger (or Morse) key is used, he places his finger lightly on it, with his hand and arm comfortably supported.

The experimenter gives the warning signal when his apparatus is ready and when the clockwork of the chronoscope has been satisfactorily started. After a nearly constant interval, preferably between one and two seconds, the stimulus is presented, either by electric means from the experimenter's room, or by the assistant who is in the subject's room. If the assistant presents the stimulus, care must be taken that the subject cannot see or hear any preparation for movement on the part of the former. In auditory reactions, the source of sound should be invisible to the subject. A dozen preliminary trials should always precede the records obtained from a hitherto unpractised subject.

The experimenter takes care that the current running through the chronoscope remains of uniform strength, as dictated by the previous experiment with the control hammer. He is careful to avoid any permanent magnetisation of the electro-magnets, by reversing the commutator after each reaction, and by allowing the current to flow through the chronoscope only when absolutely necessary. Before the first and every subsequent reaction, he takes down the times registered on the dials of the instrument. At the close of the series of reactions he subtracts successive values from one another, finds the average, the mean variation, and such other constants as are needful. If on different days a sufficient number of reactions can be obtained, a curve (or rather a polygon) may be prepared showing the distribution of individual reactions.

In 'natural' reactions the subject receives no instructions; in 'sensorial' reactions he is told to think only of the expected stimulus, and not to attend to the movement until he has received the stimulus; in 'muscular' reactions he is told to concentrate his attention on the movement with which he is about to respond, and not to think of the expected stimulus.

A series of at least ten (preferably thirty or forty) reactions should be obtained for each mode of reaction. They must be preceded by preliminary practice; and they should be followed by some further reactions, in which the subject attempts to record his mental behaviour by introspection. The difficulties of introspection may perhaps be lightened if the subject limits himself to describing in some reactions his experiences anterior to the reception of the stimulus, in others his experiences upon its reception, and in others his experiences during and after the motor response to the stimulus. (Such 'fractionisation,' however, is fraught with serious dangers.) He should specially attend to the nature of his imagery and to the part played by volition in the various forms of reaction.

(b) *Composite reactions:*

Reactions involving recognition are merely a more complete form of sensory reactions.

Reactions involving discrimination may be most easily performed by exhibiting to the subject one or other of a number of known colours and instructing him not to react until he has clearly discriminated the presented stimulus from the other possible stimuli.

Reaction times involving choice may be performed by furnishing the subject with two reaction keys, one for a finger of either hand. He is told that either a red or a blue stimulus will be exhibited, and that he is to react, say, with the right hand to red, and with the left hand to blue. In this case an assistant exhibits the stimuli, always taking care that they follow in quite irregular order, and recording the nature of the stimulus and the mode and details of the subject's response. The subject should introspectively determine his change in attitude with increasing practice.

SECTION II.

THE SPECIAL SENSES.

The first section of this course should not only have demonstrated the importance and the difficulty of introspection in connexion with psychological experiment, but should also have shown the need and the possibility of exact methods of experimentation. We now come to the second section of our study, in the course of which both of these points will receive repeated illustration. The attitude of the psychologist in dealing with the special senses must be distinguished as definitely as possible from that of the physicist and the physiologist. As psychologists, our attention throughout must be directed upon the nature of *that of which we are aware* when a sensation response takes place, and upon a determination of the conditions of that awareness. To discover 'that of which we are aware' we have to turn to introspective evidence. But the effort of introspection involved is a particularly difficult one. In every-day life sensations attract relatively little attention. They play important but, as a rule, little-noticed parts in the more complex processes of perceiving, imagining, and the like, and in the determination of our general state at any moment. Consequently, to attend to sensations, as such, demands a definite effort of abstraction.

It cannot be too strongly urged that experiments upon the special senses are of very little value from the *psychologicac* point of view, unless they are accompanied by constant and concentrated efforts of introspection. One fact which will then be found to be of the greatest general interest throughout the whole of this section, is that processes which themselves belong to an order higher than the sensory, are continually determining and modifying the nature of the sensory responses themselves and of their content. Throughout the student should consider the bearing of this upon attempts to obtain a measure of any specific kind of sensitivity. How far are such measures always relative to the general state of the subject at the time at which the measure is obtained?

In the second place, all of the experiments in this section will provide further illustration of the importance of attempting to devise exact methods. On the whole, experimental investigation has greater chance of achieving exact results in the sensory field than in any other branch of psychology. For here we can approach somewhat more nearly to the ideal of having conditions thoroughly under control and of varying them one at a time. Even in this field, however, it is certain that the experimental ideal is never more than approximately realised.

A few experiments only, from the very large number that might be attempted, have been selected for inclusion in this section. Others in the same field can better be demonstrated in connexion with lectures, and yet others require more time than can be given to them in a first year course[1], if they are to yield interesting results. The examples given have been chosen to illustrate points which bring out the type of problems and methods used by psychologists in this field of investigation.

Experiment 17.

HEAT AND COLD SPOTS.

The student should first gain a general idea of the character of the sensations produced by the stimulation of cold and heat spots. Let him successively and lightly touch neighbouring points of the skin of his hand or arm with a pencil or other cold round-pointed object, and observe how sensations of cold flash out from time to time. A round-pointed metal object, warmed in water to a temperature of about 45° C., is to be similarly moved over the skin. The blunter and more diffuse character of the sensations produced by heat spots will be at once recognised.

The experimenter now proceeds to map out an oblong area on the back of the subject's hand, measuring about 20 mm. by 10 mm. He then takes one of a number of fine copper rods of about 1 mm. in diameter which have been immersed in a vessel containing a freezing mixture of salt and ice.

---

[1] A number of these are included in Section IV of this volume.

Having dried the rod, the experimenter begins to explore the cold spots within the area above delimited. The subject sits with his eyes shut, and with his hand loosely closed and comfortably supported ; he carefully notes his experiences and records them periodically. The exploration must be done in a systematic manner, the rod being methodically applied along an imaginary series of lines, 1 mm. apart, parallel to one of the sides of the square. Along these lines the rod is lightly applied to consecutive points; it is always moved in the same direction, and where the subject exclaims that he feels a pronounced cold sensation, the experimenter marks the position of the cold spot in coloured ink or dye upon the skin, by means of a finely pointed brush. The experimenter occasionally puts back the rod into the freezing mixture, and takes up and dries a fresh one. When the area has been explored, point by point, in this way, the experimenter draws a similar area on two pieces of tracing paper, which he applies to the skin, marking in the cold spots in their proper position. One of these two records is for the subject's notebook, the other for the experimenter's.

The heat spots are to be sought for in a similar way over the same area, after the previously marked dots have been removed. These spots are fewer, but their position may readily be determined by systematically exploring the skin with a finely pointed soldering iron previously warmed in water to about 45° C. The iron may be obliquely bored with a circular hole to receive a thermometer. The advantage of using so massive an instrument lies in its long retention of the heat imparted to it. The heat spots are to be marked and their position is to be indicated, in dye or ink of another colour, upon the tracing paper used in the previous experiment.

Having selected a few exceptionally sensitive cold spots, the experimenter applies the heated point to one of them. He taps a second lightly with a very small round-pointed object, a bristle or a piece of wood. Into a third he thrusts a thin, finely pointed needle. He should take care that the stimuli both of the second and of the third spots are at th temperature of the skin. He should similarly investigate the effect of cold, touch and prick upon heat spots.

From time to time in the course of these experiments the subject must write or dictate his introspective remarks. Particularly be on the look-out for any apparent fluctuation in the efficiency of attention, or for any change of mental attitude, and note whether they have any effects upon the results.

Experiment 18.

Colour Vision.

(1) Determination of areal differences in colour sensitivity in the normal retina.

The Perimeter enables the subject to demonstrate the regions of total and partial colour 'blindness' towards the periphery of the retina, the experimenter moving towards the centre a small square of coloured paper along the free arm of the instrument. The experimenter selects such colours as orange, blue-green, or purple. He notes the points at which the colour just begins to be visible to the subject as a colourless spot. Within this zone he maps out another, in which the colour acquires a yellowish or bluish hue. Finally, he defines the innermost area, in which the colour acquires a reddish or greenish hue.

Under ordinary conditions the intermediate zone for yellow and that for blue vision are rarely quite coincident. But when care is taken that the two colours have equal chromatic and achromatic (*i.e.* brightness) values, the limits are identical. These conditions are satisfied when the two complementary coloured papers are so chosen that they require to be mixed in equal proportions to give rise to a colourless sensation, and that they are alike in size, brightness, and illumination.

An attempt should be made to find four colours which, as they are passed from the periphery over the retina, give rise (at first of course to colourless, and next) to colour sensations, the hue of which subsequently remains unaltered as the stimulus is moved still farther towards the fovea.

(2) How to test for normality of colour vision. This is best arranged as a class demonstration.

A subject may be most easily tested for colour-blindness by means of Holmgren's wools, provided that the following cautions be observed. The experimenter must never mention the name of a wool; he gives the test wool to the subject, merely asking him to select wools of similar colour. The experimenter observes not only the wools which the subject finally selects, but also those which from time to time he takes up and rejects. Weakly, as well as highly, saturated wools should be employed as test skeins, *e.g.* a very pale green (neither yellowish nor bluish) and a very pale pink, of complementary hue.

The objections to Holmgren's wools as a test of colour-blindness consist principally in the large area of the stimulus and in the neglect of the factor of varying illumination. There is reason to believe that colour-blindness, like colour-weakness, is only relative; provided that the stimulus is only of adequate area or intensity, its colour may be seen even by the colour-blind. Those who have defective colour vision may elude detection owing to their ability, through long experience, to recognise and to name colours on the basis of saturation and brightness. It may be only when the colours are viewed under abnormal illumination, *e.g.* through a foggy atmosphere, that their failure is apparent.

The advantages of the wools lie in their portability, in the absence of glass, in consequence of which their colour is constant whatever be the angle from which they are viewed in relation to the incident light, and in the fact that the test skeins can be varied so that by no amount of previous 'coaching,' which otherwise is often remarkably successful, can the colour-blind subject evade detection.

The following matches have been actually made for saturated red, yellow, blue, and green stimuli by colour-blind people. Paper discs, corresponding to the right-hand side of these equations, should be rotated on the colour wheel by the student—

Scoterythrous class . . $R = 18°\ Y + 342°\ Bk$

Photerythrous „ . . $R = 102°\ Y + 258°\ Bk$

Totally colour-blind . . $\begin{cases} R = 5°\ W + 355°\ Bk \\ Y = 136°\ W + 224°\ Bk \\ G = 152°\ W + 208°\ Bk \\ B = 88°\ W + 272°\ Bk \end{cases}$

(3) Twilight-adaptation and its consequences:

(a) Relative brightness of colours in daylight and twilight:
The gradual effects of dark-adaptation by entering a dark
room should be carefully noted. In absolute darkness only
the intrinsic light of the cerebro-retinal system remains. The
nature of this light and the details occurring therein must be
carefully studied. When the darkness is less complete and
the eye has become dark-adapted, the changes in relative
brightness of different colours are readily noticeable.

The observer determines, in bright light, the value of the
grey which results from rotating fields of yellow and blue on
the colour wheel, by matching it with a grey produced by the
rotation of black and white discs on another colour wheel.
Under like conditions, he determines the grey value from
a similar fusion of red and green fields. He observes what
alterations occur in these two matches when they are viewed
in twilight by the dark-adapted eye.

The observer notes whether differences in brightness exist
in the case of two small squares of the same coloured paper,
one being fixated at the fovea, the other stimulating the
peripheral retina; first when the eye is bright-adapted,
secondly when the eye is more or less completely dark-
adapted.

(b) Foveal blindness in twilight-adaptation. The class
will go into a dark room. Each student should carefully note
any changes in his visual experience which go on during the
time which he spends in the room. On a wall are five white
spots arranged thus: o o o o o . The students will count the spots
as they appear in peripheral and foveal vision (i.e. according
as any spot is fixated or not) after adaptation to the twilight.

Experiment 19.

COLOUR VISION (*continued*).

(i) *Successive contrast:*

(*a*) The negative after-sensation. This is best arranged as a class demonstration.

A black square on a white ground is fixated for a few seconds. The eyes are then closed, or they are directed to a large uniform grey or white surface. The observer should note (i) the degree of brightness of the after-image of the square and of its background, (ii) the series of reappearances of the after-image, (iii) the degree of distinctness of the margins of the after-image of the square.

He should next fixate a white square on a black ground, and obtain the after-image on a grey, white, or black surface, making observations as before. He should note whether the margins of the after-image of the square are as distinct as in the previous experiment, and whether the duration of original fixation affects the after-image and the breadth or brightness of the halo (sometimes called the 'corona') which surrounds it.

Similar after-images should be obtained from coloured squares upon colourless grounds. Coloured after-images should also be projected on squares of complementary or other colours. The after-image of a white square on a black ground should be projected on to an orange ground. The resulting experience should be remembered in considering later the nature of black.

The blue-green after-image of a small red patch, fixated on a white background, is projected on to a black velvet background, and the brightness and saturation of this after-image is compared with that of a small blue-green patch lying on the black velvet a few millimetres away from the point of projection of the after-image. The student should consider later whether the results of the comparison are favourable to Helmholtz's theory of the cause of after-images.

(*b*) The positive after-sensation. This is best arranged as a class demonstration.

The positive after-image which follows the extinction of a bright light is carefully noted, together with the play of colours through which the waning image passes. The observer should note in what respects, besides in hue and brightness, it differs from the negative after-image.

Special care should be taken to observe the likenesses and differences of positive and negative effects, and the ways in which they seem to be related one to the other.

(ii) *Simultaneous contrast:*

A disc containing a middle zone of black and white, surrounded by a given colour, is rotated on the colour wheel. The contrast colour is most marked when the coloured and colourless surfaces are of equal brightness.

A grey paper is successively placed on different coloured backgrounds, which are equal to it in brightness. If the contrast effect is not apparent, it is immediately forthcoming when the grey surface and its adjoining background is covered with tissue paper. The contrast effect is reduced if a pencil line be now drawn on the tissue paper, corresponding to the margins of the underlying grey paper.

The observer illuminates a white opal surface simultaneously with coloured light and with colourless light from two different sources. This can be easily effected by cutting two holes in the window-shutter of a dark room and by providing them with adjustable screens of coloured and colourless glasses respectively, as in the annexed diagram (fig. 14). Between the sources of light and the opal surface an object, *e.g.* a vertically placed ruler, is interposed, so that two shadows of it are cast upon the opal surface, the one illuminated by the coloured, the other by the colourless light. A surprisingly intense contrast colour appears in the really colourless shadow, the intensity of the contrast varying with changes in the relative brightness in the two sources of light with which the white surface is illuminated.

A point is fixated on a black surface between two red strips, which are about 10 mm. apart. The after-images are projected on to another black surface. The observer should compare the effects of projection on to grey and white surfaces, and the effects of laying the original strips on a grey or a white instead of on a black surface. He should consider what theoretical explanations of these effects can be advanced.

Pieces of the same grey paper are to be placed on colourless backgrounds of different brightness. The observer notes the production of brightness contrast. He should consider how the effects of changes in the pupil can be eliminated, and whether the contrast increases or diminishes upon fixation.

[*N.B.*—In many of the above experiments the effects of contrast are complicated owing to the simultaneous action

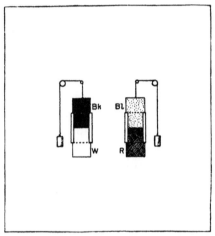

Fig. 14.

of successive contrast (due to eye movement) and owing to the knowledge that the smaller field is not an integral part of the background. The former increases, the latter diminishes the total effect. The former can be eliminated by momentary exposure, the latter by recourse to the colour wheel.]

A circular hole about 1½ inches in diameter is cut in a large white card, which is held in a horizontal position. The observer gazes through the hole on to a sheet of colourless or coloured paper placed on a table near the window. He observes the alterations in brightness of the underlying paper (*e.g.* blue or orange), which are obtained by varying the inclination of the white card.

A point is fixated on the margin between two adjoining black and white surfaces. On each surface, near the common margin, a short strip of darkish grey paper is laid. The observer notes the effect of simultaneous contrast and the changes which take place during continual fixation of the point. He should also pay attention to the relative brightness of the two strips in the after-image, bearing in mind the theories of contrast.

Experiment 20.

VISUAL ACUITY.

(a) The determination is best made out of doors on a dull cloudy day. For the E method either Snellen's illiterate test-types (fig. 15) or Cohn's arrangement (fig. 16) may be employed. The following applies to the use of the test-types.

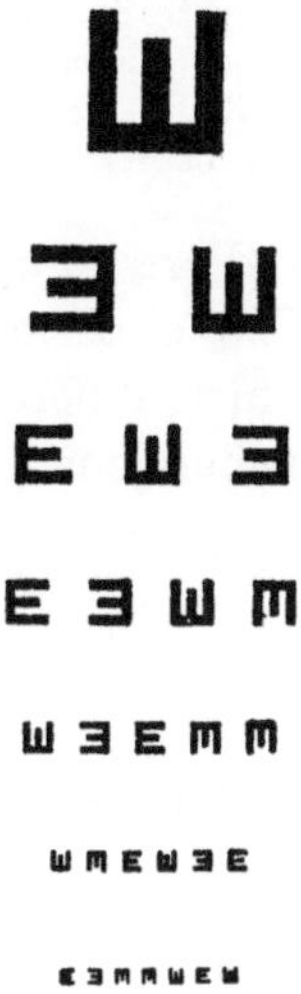

One eye of the subject is covered, while the other is tested. He stands at a distance of 15 metres from the letters. The experimenter points to the largest letters individually; the subject is asked to place in a corresponding position the E with which he is provided, or merely to state whether the open ends of the E face right, left, upwards or downwards. The experimenter proceeds from larger to smaller letters until he reaches a line in which two mistakes in ten replies occur. This is an arbitrary limit, but serves satisfactorily.

The subject is now moved a metre nearer to the letters, and the test is resumed. He advances in this way by successive metres until he can read the smallest type, known as No. 5, without making more than two mistakes in ten answers.

FIG. 15.

The visual acuity is expressed as a fraction, the numerator denoting the distance in metres at which the subject can just read a letter, the size of which is the denominator. The size of a letter is denoted by the number of metres' distance at which that letter should be read by persons possessing so-called 'normal' acuity. For such persons the numerator and denominator have the same value.

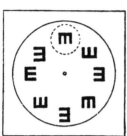

The subject must make careful introspection of his mental procedure, and of any alterations occurring therein during the investigation.

If opportunity permit, he should compare the numerical and introspective data thus obtained with those obtained by the use of such other tests of visual acuity as the laboratory possesses.

FIG. 16.—The letter *E* in various positions is drawn in black on a white card, as in the figure. This card is covered by a cardboard disc, in which a circular window is cut. By rotating the disc, the experimenter can exhibit to the subject any *E* he desires.

(*b*) A method of testing individual differences in acuity of colour vision. These differences may readily be shown in a class experiment. A number of small squares of somewhat weakly saturated colours are obtained and are set up side by side in a uniformly diffused illumination. The experimenter demonstrates the different distances at which different members of the class can distinguish the colours one from another. *No colour names should be used.*

Experiment 21.

AUDITORY EXPERIENCE.

Methods of testing acuity of hearing.

(i) The determination is best made out of doors on a still windless night. Politzer's acoumeter (fig. 17) serves as a convenient source of sound. The subject turns one ear towards this instrument, which is held between the experimenter's fingers, at a distance of five metres. The subject's other ear should be lightly stopped with cotton wool. The small percussion hammer of the acoumeter is allowed by the experimenter to fall five times at irregular intervals. He utters a warning 'Now!' before each fall, and the subject exclaims 'Yes' or 'No,' as he hears or fails to hear the sound. The subject is forewarned that sometimes no sound will be given, and the experimenter takes care irregularly to interpose five such catch experiments among every five sounds.

The experimenter increases his distance from the subject by a metre, and sounds the instrument five times, and gives five catch experiments as before. The experimenter is careful to record all the subject's answers. He continues to withdraw the instrument metre by metre in this way, until the subject fails to hear one of the five sounds. The experimenter then gives another series of five sounds and five 'catches,' at the same distance; and if another sound is missed, this distance may be arbitrarily regarded as the threshold.

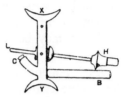

Fig. 17.—This instrument is held between the thumb and second finger at X and Y. The lever L is depressed by the fore-finger until it touches the cork C, and then it is suddenly released. By this means the metal hammer H is allowed to fall freely from a constant height on to the bar B.

The experimenter, however, should increase his distance still farther several times, and observe the resulting replies. He should then gradually bring the instrument nearer to the subject by the same stages, and observe the distance at which not more than two sounds in ten are missed by the subject.

For purposes of training in introspection, the subject should carefully observe his experiences throughout the experiment, and at the close write a full account of his results. The subject and experimenter then endeavour to correlate these results of introspection with the answers given, paying due regard to the illusions and irregularities in the subject's answers.

(ii) A group method, the sound being electrically conducted.

With this method the click produced in a pair of headgear telephone receivers, caused by the make or break of an electric circuit in which the telephones are included, is used as the source of sound. Shunted across a variable resistance are the two telephone receivers, and the experimenter uses a Morse key for the production of the test sound. Since the intensity of the sound is proportional to the amount of resistance in the circuit the latter may be used as a measure of the former. The apparatus may be readily arranged so that several sets of telephone receivers may be operated at the same time, thus making possible a group test of auditory acuity. Switches should be introduced into the circuit so that the sound may be cut out of either telephone receiver at will. In this way each ear may be tested separately as well as both ears together.

A convenient method of arranging a group test is as follows: The subjects are carefully instructed how to place the receivers on their ears. They are then told, " Immediately after you get the signal to listen you are to attend carefully and you will probably hear a series of clicks coming to the right [or left] ear. You will get a series of clicks followed by a pause, then another series of clicks followed by another pause, and finally a third series of clicks. You have to count up the number of clicks in each series and to enter the number in the space provided on the blank forms which have been given you. Each set of these clicks will give you a three-figure number. There will be five three-figure numbers to either ear." The procedure should then be carefully illustrated.

The " blank form " referred to above is most conveniently arranged as on the opposite page.

The general principle of marking the blank forms is to give 10 for each three-figure number correctly reproduced, deducting one for each click missed. But some amount of latitude must be observed. For example, a subject may return a form on which two small series of clicks have obviously been added together. He should then get credit for full marks. Thus the number 2 : 1 : 7 may be returned as 3 : 7 or as 2 : 8.

A little experience will enable an experimenter to determine the most convenient differences in intensity for him to make from one to another of the three-figure numbers. No. 1 should be presented with an intensity well above the normal threshold, and No. 5 will be well below the normal threshold.

ACUITY TEST

Name...

Date..

*Practice
Series.*

No.	3 Fig. Number
1	: :
2	• :
3	: :

No.	3 Fig. Number LEFT	3 Fig. Number RIGHT	Marks	
			L	R
1	: :	: :		
2	: :	: :		
3	: :	: :		
4	: :	: :		
5	: :	:		
TOTAL MARKS				

The whole of this experiment, if it is carefully conducted, can be made a very valuable object lesson of the uses and difficulties of group testing for psychological purposes.

4—2

(iii) Whenever possible, the group method must be supplemented by individual testing. The same instrument may be used, but instead of employing the blank forms, the subject now signals whether or not he hears the test sound as in the case of method *a*. The most convenient and least disturbing method of signalling is by means of a small flash lamp which the subject can operate with the help of a Morse key.

Experiment 22.

AUDITORY EXPERIENCE (*continued*).

(i) Identification of pitch.

This may be conducted as a group experiment. The plan of experiment is as follows:

A constant background of sound is used, and there are a series of sounds varying in pitch one from another. The subjects are first given the background consisting of a number of tones. They are then presented with one of the test sounds. This sound is given both by itself and together with the background[1]. The experimenter then instructs the subject group as follows:

" I shall give you the background of sound and keep it going throughout the whole experiment. When I say ' Now,' listen. Immediately after I may or may not switch on the test sound which you have just heard. If you think the test sound is being presented put a cross in the square on the top horizontal column of your blank form[2] which corresponds to the number of the trial given. If the test sound is absent, the appropriate square must be left blank."

At least 10 trials are given with Test Sound 1. Test Sound 2 is then added, the subjects being given adequate practice. At each 'Now' signal there are three possibilities: *i.e.* Test Sound 1,

---

[1] Most laboratories will possess materials with which this experiment can be effected. A very convenient method is to obtain a set of electrically driven vibrating forks, such as are used frequently at a telephone exchange. These can be tuned so that they give all the required variety of pitch. They remain fairly constant and are readily manipulated.

[2] This is merely a form divided into squares of an appropriate size, ten squares along each horizontal line and as many lines as there are test sounds to be used.

Test Sound 2, or no test sound. If Test Sound 1 is present the mark is a cross as before: if Test Sound 2, the mark is a small circle: if no sound is added the appropriate square is left blank. The procedure is repeated till all the Test Sounds have been used, a different symbol being employed for each Test Sound.

Score by marking errors. The score should be weighted appropriately so as to penalise most heavily the worst mistakes. A careful attempt should be made to discover on what basis the discrimination is effected.

(ii) Localisation of sound.

(a) The subject is seated blindfold in a chair, his head supported by a rest. If a 'sound perimeter' be available, the experimenter can systematically investigate the frequency and nature of the errors in localisation (i) according to the direction of the sound, (ii) according to the nature of the sound, and (iii) according to the practice of the subject.

A sound perimeter consists of a graduated metal framework, supporting the source of sound and permitting the latter to be noiselessly moved in various directions relatively to the subject.

The 'buzzer' of a telephone, carried on the perimeter, will serve as a complex sound stimulus; an electrically driven tuning-fork, driven by a distant electrically driven fork and battery, will serve as a purer tone stimulus.

The experimenter divides the horizontal and sagittal planes of space in the following manner. The subject is supposed to be seated in an imaginary sphere the centre of which lies midway between his ears. The two points on the mid-horizontal plane of the sphere, which mark the poles in front of and behind him, are regarded as 0° and 180° respectively; the two points lying to the extreme right and left of him are regarded as 90° and 270° respectively. The sagittal plane is similarly divided, 90° being the position of a point above the vertex of the subject.

In the absence of a perimeter, the accuracy of auditory localisation may be roughly investigated by four experimenters standing respectively in front of, behind and to each side of the subject, upon a graduated chalk circle about two metres in diameter, drawn on the floor. Each experimenter holds between thumb and forefinger two coins, which, when clicked, serve as the source of sound. One of the experimenters directs the movements of the others, noiselessly indicating to one or other of his colleagues that he is to give the sound at any point within his own quadrant.

In the absence of an electrically vibrating tuning-fork, two ordinary forks of identical pitch may be employed, held by separate experimenters who stand one on each side of the subject. Both forks are struck simultaneously by preconcerted signal; but, by prearrangement, one of them is damped immediately after being struck. The subject states, as before, the direction from which he supposes the sound to come. The object of striking two forks is to limit the basis of the subject's answers to sensations of tone and to exclude those of noise.

The blindfold subject verbally describes the direction from which the sound appears to come to him, and one of the experimenters carefully records the actual and the apparent direction of the sound. The following results may be expected:

(1) Fairly accurate localisation in the horizontal plane.

(2) Gross errors of localisation in the vertical sagittal plane, especially for pure tones, diminishing on practice.

(3) Tendency to confuse sounds in the horizontal plane which lie symmetrically with regard to the transverse (coronal) plane, e.g. to interpret a sound at 45° as coming from 135°.

The subject should endeavour to examine introspectively the basis of his several judgments, and from time to time he should, if possible, give the results of such introspections which are to be recorded by the experimenter beside the subject's estimations. If he finds it too difficult to attend simultaneously to the act of localisation and to the mode of localisation, a series of experiments may be subsequently conducted, in which his attention is more completely concentrated on the introspective aspect of the records, even at the expense of loss of accuracy of localisation.

At the same time, the experimenter should be on the look-out for peculiarities in the behaviour of the subject which may throw light on the psychological basis of his power of localisation.

(*b*) The influence of binaural differences of intensity should be specially investigated. A pair of headgear telephone receivers is stimulated by a single source of sound. Each receiver is shunted across a variable resistance so that the intensity of the sound to either ear can be controlled at will. The telephones should be reversed half way through the experiment.

(*c*) The influence of binaural differences of phase should be specially investigated. Read through Part I, ch. XXI, as a preliminary to this experiment.

If the forks give beats with one another, the sound will be alternately localised at different ears. Now, in the cycle between any two beats, the differences in phase between the two ears assume every possible value. Supposing that the right-hand fork is the higher, the right-hand effect will be found to follow binaural agreement in phase, the left-hand effect to follow opposition in phase.

It will also be found that, as the forks approach the ears, the localisation becomes intra-cranial, *i.e.* the sound is heard within the head.

The subject places the two ends of a long tube one in each ear, and closes his eyes, the tube resting on a table. The experimenter lightly sets a vibrating tuning-fork on the tube, along which he moves it now in one direction, now in another. The subject localises the tone intra-cranially, the tone wandering within the head from one ear to another, according to the direction of binaural difference in intensity or wave length.

The arrangement of apparatus, shown in fig. 18, enables the apparent influence of binaural phase difference upon localisation (Part I, p. 274) to be more strikingly shown. Here the tuning-fork K is applied to the open end of the T-piece, T, the long limb of which is a brass tube AB, sliding within the slightly larger tubes AC, BF. The opening T can be brought to any position of the scale DE, between 40 and 160 cm. H is the head of the subject, whose view of the position of T is prevented by the screen SS. Against his head are pressed the two padded ear caps, P and Q, which, supported on retort stands M and N, receive the sound from the tubes AC, BF. If x be the distance of T from the centre of the scale, and if λ be the wave length of the tone, the

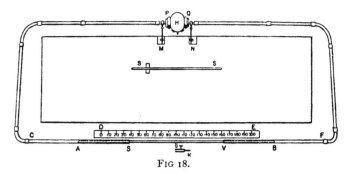

Fig 18.

tone is localised on the (experimenter's) right of the centre for values of x between 0 and $\dfrac{\lambda}{4}$, on the left of the centre for values of x between $\dfrac{\lambda}{4}$ and $\dfrac{\lambda}{2}$, and correspondingly for higher values of x.

Many subjects are able to give to such intra-cranial tones a definite localisation (*e.g.* in the pharynx or cerebellum) and can accurately describe the path of the tone as it passes from ear to ear.

Throughout the whole of these demonstrations of various sensory tests the student should notice particularly the extent and nature of the individual differences shown in the class. He should especially consider how sensory processes may appear to be affected by factors belonging to the higher mental processes.

SECTION III.

EXPERIMENTS ON PERCEPTION AND THE HIGHER THOUGHT PROCESSES.

We must now turn our attention to a field of experiment in which the difficulty of securing adequately controlled conditions is very great. We have found that all sensory processes reveal a complexity which in daily life commonly passes unnoticed. But if the sensory responses are complex, even more obviously is this the case with the higher responses of perceiving, imaging, remembering, thinking and willing. Yet we do undoubtedly gain much by the attempt to study these processes under prescribed conditions. It is true that the conditions which we are able to prescribe do not constitute all of the conditions which determine the processes we are to study. But it is better to have some conditions under control than none at all.

Moreover there is one thing which it is particularly valuable and especially difficult for the student of psychology to realise, and that is the nature of the problems with which he has to deal. There is no better way of learning what are the real problems and difficulties that beset the psychological study of the higher mental processes than to attempt experiment. Definite answers cannot in many instances be arrived at, but the definition of problems can; and that is the first step towards solution.

Throughout the whole of the work of this section the student must be continually on the look-out to see if he can improve the methods proposed. These experiments are in no sense to be regarded as cut-and-dried, or as stereotyped parts of laboratory routine. Many of them are capable of considerable extension; not a few may need amendment; but they will all throw some light upon the ways in which the student's mental processes operate.

Every opportunity should be taken to compare the results of the experiments in this section, and in several instances it will be useful to refer back to the results obtained in Section I. It is here that individual differences are most striking, and most worthy of study.

Experiment 23.

PERCEPTION OF FORM AND SIZE.

(i) *Materials required*: Pen and paper. The experimenter must prepare beforehand a set of nine simple designs, to be drawn clearly on small pieces of paper or card about 1 inch square.

The subject fixates a given spot exactly as in the case of determining areal differences of colour sensitivity (see p. 41). The experimenter chooses six of his designs. One by one, with the help of the split rod, he introduces them to his subject's peripheral vision. As soon as the form comes within his vision, the subject makes the best attempt he can to reproduce it. Afterwards the nine designs are mixed together, the subject being asked to decide which of these have *not* been presented to him.

The experiment will show clearly the defective perception of form with peripheral stimulation.

(ii) *Materials required*: Blank form of 'substitution test.' Stop watch. Pen and paper.

The student will be supplied with a sheet on which a number of different forms repeated in irregular order are printed. These will be covered, but may be momentarily uncovered one at a time. When the signal is given each student will uncover the forms, and taking each form as it comes will write down the first two letters of its name. The total time should be taken. The experiment will show the extraordinary rapidity with which the perception of form can be carried out.

(iii) *Materials required*: Set of squares cut from cardboard varying slightly in size.

1. The subject should be instructed to arrange the squares in order of ascending magnitude.

2. The experimenter should select one of the squares and place it before the subject for 10 secs. He should then remove the square, place all the other squares irregularly before the subject, and instruct the subject to choose the square next in size to the one which was presented to him. Repeat five times, noting all errors.

Compare the accuracy of perception of magnitude with the accuracy of the visual image of it.

(iv) *Materials required*: Iris diaphragm and projection lantern. The experiment consists in determining the smallest difference in magnitude of two circles exposed successively, which can be accurately discriminated. The size of the circle is determined by adjusting the aperture of the diaphragm, light through which is projected by the lantern on a screen. The effect of varying the length of exposure should be tried. This will be carried out as a group experiment.

(v) The experimenter must prepare beforehand a set of twelve cards about six inches square. The middle of each card is clearly marked by a dot which will serve as a fixation point. Towards the edge of the card but in varying positions in relation to the fixation point is printed in black a small square centimetre. Each card is, in succession, exposed momentarily to the subject, who attempts to report immediately and as exactly as possible, the direction of the square in relation to the point of fixation. The subject should try to say what factors enter into his appreciation of relative position of the square.

(vi) Make about six complex structural forms similar to those used in Section I, Experiment 3, where form, size and direction factors are all present. The subject observes these momentarily and attempts to decide in what sense, if at all, his perception of the whole can be resolved into elements of response to form, size, direction and the like.

Experiment 24.

PERCEPTION OF DISTANCE AND MOVEMENT.

(i) The material of Experiment 23 (i) is to be used, a small pin-point of light replacing the forms. Procure a number of small electric light bulbs of the kind used in an ordinary flash lamp. Mount each in a small tubular metal case containing a pin hole at one end. The case can then be mounted on the end of a split rod, leads passing from the bulb to the battery in such a way as to allow of free movement of the rod. The experimenter should first find the position at which the point of light is just visible to the subject. He then pushes the rod rapidly forward through a short, but known distance. The subject is required to make an estimate of the distance by drawing a line on paper. Ten trials to be made.

Repeat procedure with foveal stimulation.

Compare the estimates of movement seen peripherally and directly.

(ii) The following experiments deal with the relation of binocular vision and the perception of depth:

(*a*) Two similar shillings are placed, about 15 cm. apart, on a glass plate which is held close to the mid-line of the

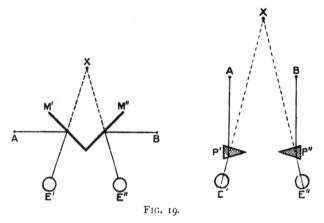

FIG. 19.

body. The image of a third single intermediate shilling can now be obtained by binocular combination, the eyes fixating a pencil point which is held (i) nearer to or (ii) further from the eyes than the two coins. The glass plate should be moved towards or away from the fixation point until binocular combination is effected. Attention should be drawn to any differences in the ease of combination and in the size or localisation of the combined image, according as the coins lie nearer to or further from the eyes than the point of fixation.

The student should familiarise himself with the theory and use of Wheatstone's mirror stereoscope and Brewster's prism stereoscope (fig. 19). Owing to the action of the mirrors, $M'M''$, or of the prisms, $P'P''$, the objects A and B are combined by the two eyes, $E'E''$, and referred to X.

(*b*) The image of a single shilling placed as before on a glass plate may be doubled, the fixation point (of a pencil) being nearer or further than the coin. The student should observe the different effect produced upon the doubled image in the two cases by closing one eye, and correlate these differences with the disparation (Part I, p. 262).

(*c*) Using the apparatus provided, the student moves the two vertical threads A and C (fig. 20) to such an extent apart that when the eyes are directed to a more distant point, on the opposite wall, the threads (one in front of each eye) yield a single combined image. Then he arranges another pair of vertical threads B and D, beside and in the same plane with the former pair, so that they also give rise to a com-

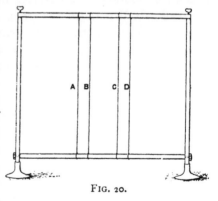

FIG. 20.

bined image. He observes now the effect of slightly increasing or decreasing the distance between B and D, so that the retinal points, excited by B and D, are no longer corresponding but disparate.

(*d*) The next experiment shows the difficulty of judging relative distance with monocular vision. Applying his eye to the end of a cardboard tube, the subject fixates a small bead, keeping the other eye closed. The experimenter drops successive beads in front of or behind the point of fixation and notes the correctness or incorrectness of the judgments given by the subject. A series of observations is then made when both eyes are open. The subject should at the same time keep an introspective record. It should be considered whether the apparatus in its rough form is altogether free from objection.

(iii) The following experiments deal with certain common illusions of movement:

(*a*) The subject makes a series of vertical marks along the smoked surface of a drum rotating on a vertical axis. He observes these marks for fifteen seconds during rotation. He then stops the drum and continues to fixate one of the marks on the smoked surface, observing the after-effects of movement.

(*b*) The subject fixates a horizontally striped black and white background, a central vertical strip of which can be set in continuous motion. He observes the apparent movement of the really fixed parts of the ground, which is set up during actual movement of the central strip, and the general reversal of movement occurring when the central strip is brought to rest.

(*c*) The subject observes the after-effects obtained after rotating on the colour wheel a white disc, on which a broad black spiral figure has been traced. The after-effects should be noted—(i) when fixation is still confined to the now resting disc, and (ii) when it is transferred to other objects.

(*d*) The subject now conceals one-half of the rotating disc by a white screen, and fixates a point on its edge, so that part of the retina receives the moving image of the half-spiral, and the other part receives the image of the stationary, screen. He observes the after-effect when the rotation is stopped.

(*e*) The subject draws a straight line $A B C D E$ (fig. 21) and divides it into imaginary quarters. He then draws a compass point slowly along the imaginary arc $F B G D H$. Fixing his regard steadily on the moving point, he observes what apparent changes take place in the direction of the line $A\ C$ as the

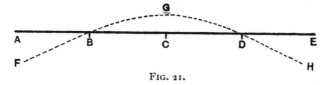

FIG. 21.

point moves from F to G, and in the direction of the line $C\ E$ as the point moves from G to H.

(f) Two dots—they may be black spots on a light field or spots of light in a dark room—are so arranged that they can be exposed momentarily in succession, separated by a controlled interval. One dot is situated below the other so that they both fall within the field of vision of the subject. When the interval separating the exposures is of a suitable length a single dot will be seen which appears to move from the one position to the other. The experimenter should investigate

(a) the influence of the rate of exposure;

(b) the influence of the position of the dots in relation to the point of fixation in monocular vision;

(c) what occurs if the dots are replaced by shapes of differing form.

Especially consider what light this experiment may throw upon the conditions of the normal perception of a moving object.

Experiment 25.

SPAN OF ATTENTION.

(i) Visual. *Materials required*: Three sets of specially prepared cards.

In Set (a) each card will contain a number of dots arranged irregularly.

In Set (b) each card will contain a number of dots arranged according to certain patterns.

In Set (c) each card will contain a number of representations of some concrete objects.

The experimenter will take set (*a*) and shuffle them thoroughly. He will then place them face downwards on the table and instruct the subject as follows:

"On each of these cards there are marked a number of dots, arranged irregularly. I will place a card before you and uncover it on the word 'Now,' covering it up again after about half a second. You are not to count the dots but to say how many dots there are on the card."

When the set is worked through, he must reshuffle the cards and repeat the procedure. Record each answer as it is given, under the index letter of the card. (The index letter: *A*, *B*, *C*, etc., will be marked on the back of each card.) Every card in the set is to be presented ten times. The percentage, extent and the nature of the errors must be worked out.

The same procedure will be followed with the two other sets. With set (*b*) the experimenter will merely say that there are dots on the cards: *i.e.*, he will not call attention to the fact that the dots are arranged in patterns. With set (*c*) the experimenter will say: "On each of these cards are a number of representations of concrete objects," etc. Note carefully any differences both in the experience and in the accuracy of estimation between the three sets.

If possible some form of tachistoscope should be employed to control exposures throughout this experiment, but this procedure is not absolutely necessary. The essentials of a good tachistoscope have been already mentioned (Part I, p. 322). Several forms of the instrument have been devised.

(*a*) In the fall tachistoscope, a screen carrying a fixation mark is allowed to drop. During its fall it momentarily exposes a card on which various objects, *e.g.* letters or figures, are arranged.

(*b*) In the rotatory tachistoscope, the subject looks down a narrow vertical blackened tube on to the periphery of a large horizontally rotating white disc, which is driven by a very steady motor. The disc has a sector cut out from its margin. The open sector allows the subject to see a card of letters, etc., placed below the disc. The rate of rotation of the disc, the area of the sector, and hence the time of exposure, can be varied at will. Fixation is secured by a preliminary trial in which an easy letter is shown in place of the card of objects.

(*c*) In the pendulum tachistoscope (fig. 22), an oblong screen *C*, provided with a central aperture, is fixed to the free end of a pendulum. The pendulum is held up by an electro-magnet, and released at the desired moment. During its swing the screen momentarily exposes the objects which lie behind it. At the end of its swing it is caught by the catch *D*. An optical arrangement can be fitted to the pendulum

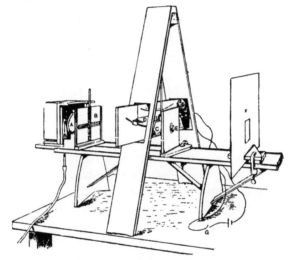

FIG. 22. Hales's Tachistoscope.

tachistoscope, by means of which the images *B* of stencilled lines, letters, or figures, placed behind the screen, can (during the momentarily favourable position of the aperture) be thrown forward by aid of the condenser *A* and the lens *E* on to a plate of ground glass at *F*, which carries a fixation mark fixated by the subject. The subject's head is supported by a head rest.

(ii) *Auditory. Materials required* : Any apparatus by means of which the experimenter can produce a given number of simple sounds in rapid succession.

This will be carried out as a group test.

The experimenter will say: "I shall give you a signal, 'Now.' There will immediately follow a number of sounds in rapid succession "—he will here give a few illustrations—" On each occasion, without counting the sounds separately, you have to try to record the number in the group."

Several practice trials should be given.

Results are to be worked out as in the case of the visual span.

Experiments 26 and 27.

PROCESSES OF IMAGING.

(i) *Materials required*: Set of five or more pictures alike in certain respects, but different in other respects. These will be provided. Stop-watch.

The experimenter will place the cards face downwards on the table, and will say:

"On each of these cards is a picture. When I give you the signal, take up a card and look at it carefully, noting all the details you can. You will be given fifteen seconds for each card. When I say 'Time,' put down the card and be ready for the signal to take up the next one."

As soon as the set is worked through, put it aside and go on at once with experiment (ii).

(ii) *Materials required*: Pen and paper. Stop-watch.

This is best carried out as a class experiment. The experimenter will say: "When I give you the signal, begin at once and write down a list of objects all of which are of a particular colour (naming the colour). You will have five minutes for the work." As soon as the list is completed, the subject must work through it, giving particular attention to the type of imagery which may have accompanied the writing down of the words.

Similar lists will now be compiled for *sounds*, for *tastes*, and for *touch*.

The subjects will now return to experiment (i). Each will write a description of the pictures seen, in what he believes to be the correct order, and with as much detail as possible.

Special effort is to be made to *visualise* the cards. Any other imagery occurring should be noted. *The cards are not to be seen again.*

(iii) *Materials required*: Three sets of letter squares. These must be prepared beforehand. The letters are to be printed clearly and in capitals, on a square about half the size of an ordinary post-card. The size of the letters should be such that they may be read without difficulty by any person with normal vision at his usual reading distance. They are to be placed in four rows, four in a row. Any order may be adopted, but care should be taken to see that the order of the letters does not facilitate memory. Consonants only are to be used. For example:

$$
\begin{array}{cccc}
B & M & J & X \\
V & G & L & P \\
Q & D & S & J \\
C & F & W & H \\
\end{array}
$$

The experimenter will place the first letter-square before the subject and instruct him as follows:

"On this card are a number of consonants, four rows, four in a row. When I say 'Now,' turn over the card and, *as far as possible inhibiting the use of names*, attempt to learn the letter-square."

Make quite sure that the subject understands exactly what he has to do. Allow 10 seconds for learning. Then say: "Now put the card aside, and start counting aloud 1 to 20." Keep the subject doing this for 20 secs. Then give him a blank sheet. Say: "Now try to reproduce the letter square. As far as possible you are to use visual imagery only."

Take the second square. Say: "On this card etc.... When I say 'Now' turn over the card, and read the letters aloud, taking the square in horizontal rows. You will be given 10 secs." Complete the procedure as before. This reproduction is as far as possible to be made on the basis of auditory and motor imagery.

Take the third square. Say: "On this card etc.... When I say 'Now,' turn over this card and read the letters to yourself, at the same time uttering aloud the vowel sound 'Ah—h'."

You will be given 10 secs. Complete the procedure as before. (See Part I, pp. 138–9.)

(iv) *Materials required*: Three sets of ten ink blots, five black and five coloured[1].

(*a*) The experimenter says: "I have a number of ink blots here. They represent nothing in particular, but they may remind you of some object, just as cloud-shapes often do, or as you may see 'faces in the fire.' I shall expose the cards one by one. Write down the first thing that comes into your mind when you see the cards, and record also the type of imagery in which the suggestion appears."

The cards are best set up at a distance of five or six feet from the subject, and each card should be exposed for not more than one minute. All suggestions, or the absence of suggestions should be recorded.

(*b*) The experimenter says: "I have here a second set of blots. I will set them up and I wish you to record suggestions as before. This set, however, is generally supposed particularly to suggest living creatures and movement."

At the end of this experiment the subject should be asked to compare his attitude to this set with that which he adopted to set (*a*). If there are any changes in the nature of the images which appear they should be carefully noted.

(*c*) The experimenter must select beforehand some short piece of highly imaginative poetry or prose; *e.g.* passages from Coleridge, or de Quincey, or E. A. Poe, or W. de la Mare. He says: "Before we proceed with the next experiment I want you to read the following." The subject reads the passage and is asked to make any comment he pleases. Special note should be made of any images which are reported to occur.

(v) Now return to experiment (i) and if possible get a further description of the pictures. Carefully compare the description with the original pictures and attempt to analyse the nature of the errors.

---

[1] Suitable blots may be easily made. A few spots of ink are scattered on a piece of paper with a fairly absorbent surface. The paper is then folded across and pressed so that the ink spreads.

Throughout these experiments the following questions are to be kept in mind:

1. What is the significance of individual differences both as regards vividness and as regards type of images?

2. What are the main functions of imagery, and do these differ according to the type of imagery employed?

3. What are the main lines of change which images may undergo with lapse of time, and what are the chief conditions determining such changes?

4. In what ways do the nature and type of imagery depend upon the attitude of the subject?

5. Is imagery liable to be determined by suggestion?

Experiment 28.

MEMORY: METHODS OF EXPERIMENT[1].

Before coming to the class the student should read carefully Part I, chapter XII.

(i) *The Saving method:* Materials required: Lists of non-sense syllables, pen and paper.

Each member of the class prepares a series of twelve senseless three-letter syllables, taking care—

(*a*) that two consecutive syllables do not form a sensible word;

(*b*) that the same vowel is not repeated in two consecutive syllables;

(*c*) that no two letters of one syllable recur in another syllable of the same series;

(*d*) that the final letter of one syllable is not the initial letter of the next.

These syllables are to be written out in large printed characters, one beneath the other, each series on a separate sheet of paper, which is then handed by the writer to his neighbour. At a given signal each person begins silently

---

[1] An elementary class cannot be expected to give sufficient time to experiment and to preliminary practice, in order to obtain quantitative results of any value. They should, however, familiarise themselves with the experimental methods.

to learn the series by the learning method. A noiselessly swinging pendulum (or a metronome) ensures a constant rate of reading. At the first correct reproduction the experiment is stopped. The repetitions are counted at the close of the experiment by observing the number of discs of cardboard, one of which is dropped from the hand of the subject after each repetition. After a given interval, say one hour, the series is relearnt as before, and the saving in repetitions is noted.

The interval between learning and relearning may be well filled by an experiment on serial reproduction. This is a group experiment and the material must be prepared by the demonstrator. For each member of the class a fairly simple line drawing is prepared, as, for example, of a house, of some animal, or of an Oriental mask. The experiment will be the more instructive if the drawing contains some rather unusual features, as in the case of the Oriental face. The experimenter distributes to each member of the class his particular representation, which the subject studies for a prescribed period, thereafter attempting a reproduction. The reproduction is passed by the subject to his neighbour in the class who in the same way effects a reproduction which he passes to the next subject. This procedure is repeated until each member of the class has participated in the chain of reproductions obtained from each starting point. All the reproductions are subsequently analysed. They will be found to yield many interesting illustrations of the progressive changes which co-operative reproduction often bring about in actual life.

A similar experiment may be carried out with verbal material. Short anecdotes, or extracts from folk stories provide particularly interesting material.

Experiment 29.

MEMORY (*continued*).

(ii) *The Scoring method.*

The following is Müller's arrangement of apparatus for this method. The student should familiarise himself with the use of such instruments as the laboratory possesses, which are available for the purpose, should the laboratory not possess the apparatus which is here described.

In this method the syllables are written on a cylinder, and during the rotation of the cylinder on its horizontal axis they are successively exposed to the subject before a small window in a screen. During reading, the subject gives, so far as possible, equal attention to each syllable, and accents them as directed. In the interval between the last reading and the re-exhibition, he is careful to avoid thinking over his lesson.

The re-exhibition apparatus consists of a polyhedral prism, rotating on a horizontal axis, on each side of which is printed the first syllable of some pair belonging to the series of syllables already learnt. This prism is concealed from the subject's eye by a releasable screen, which falls when the subject breaks an electric circuit, thereby exposing a single syllable printed on the presented side of the prism. By closing another electric circuit, the falling screen sets a Hipp's chronoscope in action at the moment of exposure of the syllable. The subject, in giving out his reply, stops the movement of the chronoscope owing to its electrical connexion with a lip key or a voice key which moves when he speaks. The chronoscope readings, thus obtained for the various pairs of syllables, are indeed not identical with, but they may be taken as a measure of, the time occupied in reviving the associated syllable.

(iii) *Economical methods of learning.*

The experimenter writes in a clear hand a dozen verses of poetry on the blackboard. The subjects note the number of silent repetitions necessary to learn them by the entire method, counting the repetitions, as in Exp. 28, by dropping, as before, a small disc of cardboard from the hand at each repetition. After five minutes' rest, the number of necessary repetitions is determined in order to learn a further series of equally difficult verses by the sectional method, the series being learnt in two equal sections. After similar intervals, a third series is learnt by the entire method, a fourth series by the sectional method, in which the series is divided into three (four, or six) sections, and a fifth series by the entire method.

The class should compare the economy in repetitions for these three methods, and make careful introspective records of their experiences. They should consider what further factors need to be investigated, in order to determine more accurately the relative economy of methods of learning.

Experiment 30.

MUSCULAR AND MENTAL FATIGUE.

(i) *Muscular fatigue.*

The dynamometer and the ergograph are two instruments which have been used in the psychological study of muscular fatigue. Observations have generally been confined to local, they have not extended to general, bodily fatigue.

The dynamometer registers the squeeze or pull of the hand or finger against a steel spring. It may be used in two ways: either to record the maximal force of a momentary muscular contraction under varying conditions, or to record the variations in that force when prolonged effort is made to maintain a state of maximal contraction. The instrument, however, has various drawbacks. In the first place, the maximal force varies with the suddenness with which the contraction is made. Secondly, the pressure of the bar or handle against the skin is apt to be very painful, and therefore to inhibit the full force of the contraction. Thirdly, the movement required is so complex that there is no security against bringing into use different muscles, or against contracting different muscles to varying extents, at different times in the course of the investigation. A modified form of the dynamometer is employed and figured in Exp. 51.

The ergograph (fig. 23) is especially adapted for the study of simple movements in which very few muscles are involved. The most usually studied movement consists in extending and flexing the middle finger. It is the essence of a good instrument that, by the rigid fixation of the arm, hand, and other fingers, all auxiliary movements be, so far as possible, excluded, and that a minimum of discomfort attend the

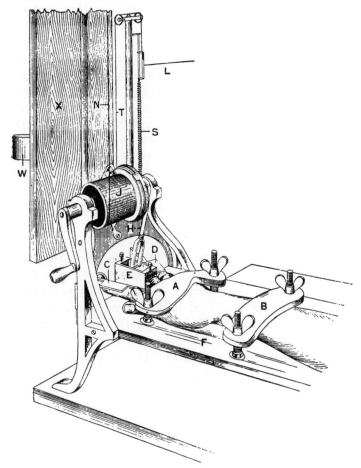

FIG. 23. Kräpelin's Ergograph.

recording of the ergogram. In most instruments the work is done (that is to say, the weight is lifted) with the hand placed palm upwards; in others (cf. fig. 23) the hand rests with the palm downwards.

In Kräpelin's ergograph (fig. 23) the arm is placed on a firmly fixed platform F, and is clamped by the cross-bars A and B. The middle finger lies midway between the first and third fingers, which are separated from it by the right-angled plates C and D. It is comfortably but firmly secured by means of screws within the box E, and is free to execute upward and downward movements. The several parts which thus fix the fingers are movable and are graduated, so that the hand can be repeatedly replaced in the same position. The movements of the middle finger are communicated by the steel ribbon H to the axis of J, and thence by the cord T to the lever L, which is raised against the action of the spring S. L records the finger movements on a travelling smoked surface. The upright board X is 10 feet or more in height. At its top it bears a pulley, round which passes a long wire, attached at one end N to the spirally grooved surface J, and at the other end to the (variable) weight W placed on the other side of the board.

Flexion of the middle finger rotates J, and thus raises W, but the axis of J is so arranged that no reverse movement of J or lowering of W occurs during relaxation of the finger. In virtue of this contrivance, it is easy to calculate the total height to which W has been raised during any experiment, by means of a vertical scale placed on the rear surface of X.

In a series of preliminary experiments, the weight which has to be raised must be regulated according to the physique of the subject and according to the prescribed frequency of movement.

To obtain an ergogram of the usual form, as shown in Part I, fig. 4, the weight must be relatively heavy. A metronome is used to mark the rate of rhythm. The subject's eyes are screened from the smoked surface, on which the height and number of his contractions are recorded. When the height and number of the contractions, or the total height through which the weight has been lifted in a known time, are known, the amount of work can readily be expressed in units of work (kilogram-metres).

(ii) *Fatigue and co-ordination of movements.*

The student should familiarise himself with some form of dotting or aiming test. In the former a strip of paper is passed before the subject at a constant speed. On the paper are a number of small circles in slightly varying positions. As each circle passes before him, the subject attempts to mark its exact centre with a pencil.

In the latter, blank forms may be used on each of which are a number of sets of concentric circles, a mm. space between the circumference of each circle. With a small needle pointer, working at a regular speed and in an assigned direction, the subject endeavours to spear a hole in the centre of each concentric set. By an arrangement for removing and setting up blank forms at the appropriate times a subject may be kept at work for long periods.

As muscular and mental fatigue increase precision of aim diminishes.

(iii) *Mental work.*

The student must first read Part I, pp. 178–81.

The chief difficulty of the 'completion,' 'letter-erasing,' and 'learning' tests lies in evaluating the results. The errors may be either of commission or of omission, and it is not easy to apportion the 'bad marks' which each kind of error should deserve. Some investigators allow only half a bad mark to an error of transposition in the learning test; others graduate the mark according to the extent of transposition.

In the completion test, it is essential that the material should be of constant interest and difficulty for different subjects, and for the same subject at different times. An approach to uniformity may be attained by confining the omitted words to some definite part of speech, *e.g.* to verbs.

In the letter-erasing tests, the material should again be of constant interest and familiarity. This ideal is best reached in the case of adults by using nonsense words, or in the case of children by using a foreign language which is known to be absolutely meaningless to them. If pages of nonsense words are specially prepared, it is well to arrange the words so that every half page contains a constant number of examples of the letter which the subject is enjoined to erase.

The methods employed in the learning test have been already discussed (Part I, pp. 144–7).

For the simple addition of the calculation tests, special books of figures (*Rechenhefte*) have been prepared under Kräpelin's direction. The subject adds each figure to the next and writes down the result. He then starts afresh and adds the next pair of figures, and so on. He makes a mark at the figure reached whenever the time signal is sounded.

These books are not so suitable for multiplication, as special arrangements are necessary so that the various pairs of figures multiplied shall be of fairly uniform difficulty.

Satisfactory experimental results can hardly be expected from students whose opportunities for investigation are confined to the hours of class laboratory work. In a few initial experiments it is impossible to eliminate the enormous influence of accommodation and practice. Nevertheless, the student cannot be too strongly urged to familiarise himself with some, at least, of the methods described in the text, and to preserve a record of his introspections made after submitting himself to the tests.

The forms required for any of the above tests may now be obtained from practically any educational publisher who is interested in mental tests.

Experiments 31 and 32.

MENTAL TESTS.

The class will work as a group through two or three selected sets of mental tests. Convenient sets for adult classes are Ballard's Chelsea and Crichton Mental Tests[1]. But widely used sets such as the Terman *Group Tests of Mental Ability*[2], the *Northumberland Mental Tests*[2], and the like should also be employed. Test answers should be marked by the class, and especial attention should be given to the precautions which have to be observed in giving and marking mental tests.

[1] Published by Hodder and Stoughton: London.
[2] Harrap and Co.: London.

SECTION IV.

The experiments included in this section may be regarded as supplementary to those already described, or they may be made the basis of a second year's course. In the latter case, the leader of a class should diversify and add to them as his own judgment and the resources of his laboratory direct He should in every instance strive to get a much more thorough discussion both of methods and of results than is possible during a first year's work.

Experiment 33.

CUTANEOUS AND THERMAL SENSATIONS.

(*a*) *Touch spots.* A convenient set of instruments for demonstrating the existence of touch spots can be made by perpendicularly mounting hairs of different lengths and thicknesses, each at the end of a match. The pressure exerted by a hair depends chiefly on its length and thickness, and within wide limits is independent of the extent to which it is bent. This pressure may be measured in grams, by applying the end of the hair to one of the scales of a balance.

The experimenter carefully notes the points of emergence of all the hairs within the area of the subject's skin already delimited. He marks these points on the skin in ink and transfers them to a corresponding square of tracing paper, as before. A magnifying-glass should be used to detect the finer, shorter, or fairer hairs. Then the hairs are cut off by fine scissors close to the skin surface, and the dots are washed away. (If the hairs were not cut off, it would be impossible to explore the cutaneous area satisfactorily. The hairs would frequently be touched by accident, and would as often stimulate the underlying touch spot.) The experimenter selects a mounted hair which provides a stimulus of suitable strength, and explores the area systematically by a series of steady touches as before, the long axis of the hair being always applied perpendicularly to the skin. A few preliminary experiments should be made to acquaint the subject with the peculiar sensation produced by a touch spot. Each touch spot is to be marked on the skin in coloured ink, and when the whole area has been explored, the dots are to be transferred to the paper square; their relation to the original position of the hairs, and their independence of the position of the temperature spots being noted. The subject should observe the variations in character of the sensation produced by touch spots of different sensitivity. He should note whether any other sensations than those of touch are simultaneously or subsequently produced, and he should observe the differences in accuracy of localisation and in the apparent depth of the sensations produced by the temperature and touch spots.

(*b*) *Pain spots*. Let the experimenter lightly touch the bent knuckle of a finger of the subject with a finely pointed object, *e.g.* a needle. It is easy to observe that at certain spots the distinctly localised touch sensation is followed, after an obvious interval, by a more radiating, ill-localised and unpleasant sensation of pain.

The experimenter should endeavour to discover pain spots in a small part of the hairless area already used in the previous experiment. Care must be taken that the needle never pierces the skin. For this reason it is preferable to use pointed horse hairs or bristles, the sensitivity of the pain spots being raised by a thorough softening of the skin with soap and warm water. The advantage of pointed hairs lies in the possibility of standardising their pressure.

The experimenter selects (*a*) a touch spot which has not a pain spot in its immediate neighbourhood, and (*b*) a pain spot which has not a touch spot in its immediate neighbourhood. He stimulates each of them, and observes whether the double sensation of touch and pain obtained above is present.

The inside of the cheek is explored by the point of a needle or by the interrupted current from an induction coil, the subject satisfying himself as to the existence of a painless area. The internal surface of the mouth will be found throughout to be less sensitive than the skin to pain.

The hand is dipped into water at 50° C.   The initial sensation of temperature, preceding that of pain, is observed.

(*c*) *Temperature sensations.* If the entire hand be dipped into water at 25° C., and if one finger of the other hand be dipped into water which is a few degrees higher in temperature, it will be observed that within certain limits, increase of the extent of surface stimulated causes increase in the intensity of the temperature sensation.   Similarly, water which is not uncomfortably warm to a small area of the body becomes intolerably painful when a larger surface is immersed.

N.B.—It will be observed that when the arm is immersed in water (or, better, in mercury) no sensation of pressure is produced save at the line of emergence of the arm from water. The student should consider any possible explanation of this observation.

The subject places a finger of one hand in water at 15° C., and the corresponding finger of the other in water at 40° C. He notes the gradual changes in sensation, and after a few minutes he transfers the two fingers to water at 28° C., in which he moves them about, observing the temperature sensations in each of the fingers.

N.B.—The student should consider how it is that there is a difference between the temperature sensations afforded by touching various objects, solid and liquid, rough and smooth, about the room; and why it is that the same room feels warmer after a walk on a windy day, than after a walk on a windless but equally cold day.

The subject places the same two fingers respectively in water at 45° and 28° C., the latter representing approximately the normal temperature of the skin.   After about fifteen seconds he transfers the fingers to water at 10° C., in which he moves them about.   How can the fact be explained that the coldness of the latter is at first less felt by the finger which had been previously immersed in the hotter water? The experiment may be varied by transposing the two vessels of water at 10° and 45° C.

The subject places a cold coin (about 5° C.) on his palm or forehead for about half a minute, and observes the after-sensation following removal of the coin. Is it continuous throughout or ever intermittent? Does it differ in any way from the character of the cold sensation? Similarly, the subject observes the after-sensation following removal of a warm object. He should consider the bearing of the two experiments on Weber's and Hering's theories. He should then investigate the after-effects of a stimulus applied for two minutes and maintained at about 9° C.

The subject compares the weights of two similar coins placed alternately on the palm (or forehead), the one coin having been previously cooled, the other having been warmed approximately to the temperature of the skin. It will be found that the illusion holds for objects which are above as well as for those which are below the skin temperature.

Experiment 34.

LABYRINTHINE AND MOTOR SENSATIONS.

(a) *Labyrinthine sensations.* The movements and after-sensations which occur after passive rotation may be studied by first turning the subject seated blindfold[1] on a turn-table through ten revolutions at a uniform speed of two revolutions per second. (The chair in which the subject sits should be provided with rests for the arms, feet and back, and should be firmly fixed to the turn-table.) The turn-table is then stopped as suddenly as possible. The subject is at once helped to his feet and stands with his feet together, the experimenter having his hands ready for support, if necessary. The three pairs of canals may be separately investigated by varying the inclination of the head during rotation, the external (horizontal) canals being principally stimulated in the erect position of the head, the superior canals when the face is directed upwards or downwards, the posterior canals when the head is laterally inclined to one shoulder. Thus in the case of the external canals the post-rotatory effects are

---

[1] For the convenience of studying the eye-movements, opaque spectacles may be worn.

(i) irresistible bodily movements of the subject causing him to rotate circus-wise in the direction of the previous passive rotation, and (ii) a horizontal nystagmus (rapid oscillation) of the eyes when they are turned towards the direction opposite to that of the rotation. These bodily and ocular movements will be found to differ in plane and character according to the canals stimulated, *e.g.* the superior canals evoking lateral flexion, the posterior canals dorso-ventral flexion, of the body.

Another method of investigating the sensations of the labyrinth is by the 'caloric' reaction. If one ear be slowly irrigated with tepid water while the head of the subject is held erect, giddiness begins after a short interval, and if the irrigation be then stopped, the giddiness continues and despite instructions to stand steady the subject irresistibly executes forced movements of the head, often of the body and limbs also, towards the side opposite to the ear irrigated. When the eyes are directed to this opposite side, a rotatory nystagmus is produced. Hot water in place of tepid water will be found to yield precisely opposite effects, apparently owing to reversal in direction of the convection currents of the endolymph. The external canals may be investigated by the same method with face downwards. The deep-seated position of the posterior canals apparently makes them insusceptible to the effects of heat or cold.

Full introspective data should be supplied by the subject throughout the above experiments.

(*b*) *Passive movement and resistance.* The subject's arm is bared and supported in a comfortable resting position. His eyes are closed. The experimenter places on the forearm a weight, the base of which is covered with a pad of blotting paper, in order to reduce the conduction of heat from the skin. He leaves it there for several seconds. The subject records the various experiences which he obtains during and after the application of the weight. After allowing a sufficient interval of rest, the experimenter next applies a much heavier or lighter weight to the subject's arm, and a similar introspective record is obtained.

The same experiment is performed while the skin is being rendered anæsthetic by spraying it with ether. The skin is

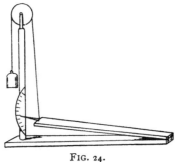

sprayed for about half a minute, and then the weight is placed upon it for a few seconds. Thereupon the weight is removed and the spraying is recommenced. This alternation is continued until the skin is quite anæsthetic. Careful introspective records—and these are easily procurable after a little training—will

FIG. 24.

yield interesting points of comparison with the records obtained in the previous experiment.

The effects of passive movement may be roughly studied by means of the apparatus illustrated in figure 24. The subject's forearm is laid on the hinged board, which is moved by the experimenter pressing down the counterweight. It is easy to observe that sensations of tension precede those of movement, and that the latter sensations may occur although the subject is unable to determine the direction of movement.

A finger of the subject's hand is fitted with a band, to which is attached a thread carrying a weight. The subject, blindfolded, holds his arm horizontally away from the body, and proceeds slowly to lower the arm. Meanwhile the experimenter suddenly and noiselessly removes the weight. The subject will note the sensation of resistance and the tendency to upward movement of the limb. He should carefully record these and other experiences occurring during the experiment, and he should endeavour to interpret them in the light of his knowledge of motor sensations.

(*c*) *Threshold for appreciation of movement.* For accurately studying the limen or threshold of just perceptible active or passive movement in different joints, apparatus must be so contrived as to permit of movement only in the joint which is under consideration. Thus, in studying the movement of a finger joint, the palm and the remaining fingers are steadied in a plaster mould, and are kept at rest by the pressure of cushions, while the other joints of the finger are securely fixed. Under such conditions, the finger may be passively moved by means of a finger-cap fitting on to the tip of the finger, a thread passing from this cap over a pulley and terminating in a (variable) weight. A lever may be attached to the thread and brought to bear on a travelling smoked surface, whereby the extent and speed of the movement of the finger, whether it be moved actively or passively, may be recorded.

Such an experiment is too complicated for class work. On the other hand, the apparatus for studying appreciation of differences in extent of movement may be of a quite simple character. A graduated ruler, to which a rider and a stop can be fixed, will indeed suffice. A more convenient form of the apparatus (fig. 25) consists of a little trolley T made to receive the finger at F. This trolley travels easily along rails laid upon a graduated board, which can be placed in any position. The subject, standing or seated conveniently before the apparatus with his eyes closed, places his finger in the trolley, and his arm executes actively or passively the desired movement. A string, pulley P, and weight may be attached to the trolley, so as to increase or decrease the necessary force of movement. The excursions of the trolley can be limited in either direction by the movable stops S', S''.

With such an apparatus, the arm of a blindfold subject may be actively or passively moved to a known extent, from a known position, in a known direction, with a known speed. And after a known interval of time the subject, still blindfold, may be asked to make an apparently equally extensive movement, from the same, or from a different, original position of the arm, with the same or with the opposite arm, in the same or in a different direction, with the same or with a different speed: and the accuracy of his estimate is recorded. Or, after a known interval, the subject's arm may be passively moved in a pre-determined manner, and his judgment in comparing the extent of the two movements recorded. Or again, two such trolleys may be prepared, so that the effects

6—2

and the comparison of simultaneous movements of the two arms may be investigated.

It is obvious that a great variety of psychological experiments can be performed in this simple way. But the conditions

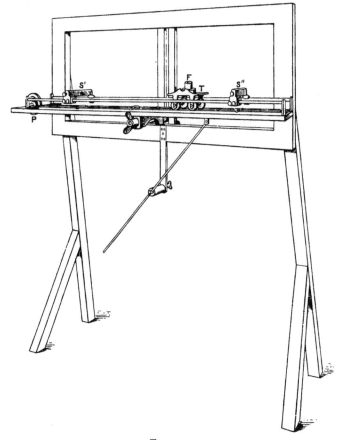

FIG. 25.

laid down in chapter XV must be scrupulously observed. The student is therefore advised to postpone working for the present with this apparatus.

One defect of such an instrument is that it provides no means of insuring a constancy of the share which the different joints (*e.g.* the finger, the wrist, the elbow, and the shoulder) take in each total movement. Another objection is that it does not eliminate the complicating effects of sensations of cutaneous and deep pressure. With practice, however, a sufficiently uniform movement is attained. And it has the advantage of being a movement comparable to the movements made in everyday life.

Experiment 35.

GUSTATORY SENSATIONS.

(*a*) *Reactions of individual papillæ.* The experimenter makes a rough outline of the subject's tongue, sketching in any striking landmarks (ridges, etc.) which will serve to locate individual papillæ. He selects six prominent, easily identifiable papillæ, preferably in different situations, and notes their position on the map of the tongue.

He dries the subject's tongue with a piece of cloth or cotton wool, and investigates the reaction of these papillæ to distilled water and to sweet, bitter, salt, and sour solutions. The solutions are to be applied by means of fine brushes, which are kept in water and are dried before being dipped in the solutions. A lens should be used by the experimenter in order to insure exact application to the papillæ. The experimenter lightly applies the brush to the papilla for two seconds. The subject does not withdraw his tongue until he has an answer ready. The papillæ are tested, and the solutions are employed, in irregular order. A brief rest, preceded by rinsing the mouth, follows each application of the brush.

Record is made of (i) the time elapsing between application of the stimulus and development of the sensation, (ii) the duration of the sensation, (iii) the nature of the sensation, (iv) any changes in its character.

The experimenter paints a papilla, which is sensitive to all four tastes, with a 10 per cent. solution of cocaine. He tests it with taste solutions, repeating the painting and testing until no further effect is obtained.

N.B.—Care must be taken not to apply cocaine to a wide surface of the subject's tongue, as some individuals are peculiarly susceptible to the dangerous effects of too much cocaine.

After the subject has chewed some gymnema leaves, or after an already tested papilla has been painted with a solution of gymnemic acid, the experimenter again tests the reaction of the papilla.

(*b*) *Mixture, compensation and rivalry.* Two different taste solutions are mixed and applied to a papilla which is sensitive to the two tastes. Both weak and strong solutions should be tested, and the presence of compensation, rivalry, or of an altogether new sensation, be investigated.

(*c*) *Contrast.* Having dried the subject's tongue, the experimenter applies to one side of it two drops of a taste solution of the nature of which the subject must be quite ignorant. The solution must at first be so weak that the tasting substance is incapable of stimulating the end organs. It is applied to the tongue by means of a finely pointed glass tube. The solution is to be increased in strength until with successive applications the subject gives correct replies. The subject continues to hold out his tongue after every application, until a taste sensation is developed or until the lapse of time has assured him that no sensation is likely to arise. In every case the experimenter notes down the subject's replies. The subject rinses his mouth with water when this part of the experiment is finished, and rests a while.

The experimenter now attempts to induce simultaneous contrast by applying to the opposite side of the subject's tongue two drops of a fairly strong solution of another taste (the inducing taste), while on the other side he applies drops of the taste solution previously used, starting, however, with pure distilled water and gradually increasing the strength of the tasting substance until its taste is recognised. The solutions should be dropped on the two sides of the tongue as nearly simultaneously as possible. Care must be taken that they do not mingle on the tongue.

The effects of successive contrast may be demonstrated

by applying the inducing taste solution to the tip of the tongue. After two or three seconds the tongue is withdrawn and the mouth is well rinsed. The experimenter then applies various strengths of a weak previously imperceptible taste solution to the same area.

Experiment 36.

OLFACTORY SENSATIONS.

(*a*) *Classification of smells.* The subject should familiarise himself with the smells of odorous substances which are at his disposal. He should note whether tactile, painful, thermal, or gustatory concomitants of the olfactory sensation are present in each case; and how far he agrees with Zwaardemaker's classification.

(*b*) *Respiration and smell.* The subject takes several rapid deep inspirations and expirations, so that he is subsequently able to hold his breath for about twenty seconds. As soon as he starts holding his breath he closes his eyes, and brings before the nose a bottle of strong ammonia or of spirits of camphor. He observes the pricking sensation and the entire absence of olfactory sensation. When the breath can no longer be held, he closes the nostrils with the fingers, removes the bottle, and takes ever so gentle an inspiration, observing the change in sensation.

(*c*) *Olfactory fatigue.* The subject familiarises himself with the character and intensity of the odours of chlorine water, animal musk, copaiba balsam, heliotropin, and ether. He plugs one nostril with cotton wool and holds under the other a bottle containing spirits of camphor, or ammonium sulphide, or tincture of iodine. With eyes closed he continues smelling the bottle until the odour is no longer perceived. Then he examines the five odours above named and determines whether or not they have changed in character or intensity. He compares the different results according as the nose has been exposed to spirits of camphor, ammonium sulphide, or tincture of iodine.

The subject should observe the gradual changes in sensation, as nitrobenzol, oil of camphor, or heliotropin is persistently smelled.

(*d*) *Mixture, compensation, rivalry.* By using a double form of Zwaardemaker's Olfactometer (Part I, fig. 8), the effects of simultaneously presenting two odours to the nose may be accurately studied. For class purposes, however, it may suffice for the experimenter to take two bottles containing the odours and to pass them repeatedly in rapid succession before the nostrils while the subject is taking a slow prolonged inspiration. The subject must be already quite familiar with the separate odours, so that he may observe whether from time to time an altogether new sensation occurs when they are presented together.

Experiment 37.

VISUAL SENSATIONS.

(*a*) *Characters of colourless and colour sensations.* The series of colourless sensations obtained by varying the proportions of black and white upon the colour wheel (fig. 26) should be carefully observed[1].

The saturation of a colour is to be changed by mixing with it on the colour wheel varying amounts of grey or white. The results of mixing colours with black should be also observed, and subsequently reconsidered in their relation to the theories of colour vision.

The varying brightness of differently coloured papers should be noted. The degrees of brightness are to be determined by comparing them with papers of the colourless series. If the black-white values of the latter be known, the brightness of the various colours may be expressed in terms of these values; thus

$$Y = 178° W + 182° Bk.$$

[1] When papers are mounted on the colour wheel, an *uncut* paper disc of the same diameter must always be placed behind them. Before the nut is screwed on, a minute disc of thick paper, having the same diameter as that of the nut, is interposed, in order to prevent the pressure of the latter from marking and wearing out the papers. Care must be taken to arrange the papers and to turn the colour wheel in a direction so that the free edges of the papers lie flat during rotation; otherwise, by flying up, they will become torn.

The student should be in a position to answer for himself the question, How may the saturation of a colour be changed upon the colour wheel, while its brightness remains unaltered?

The observer sets up two squares of equally white papers at different distances from a window, one behind the other, so that when he looks at them with one eye directed through an open tube he obtains a circular plane field, filled half with the one and half with the other paper. Having set the papers at a distance from one another, which is just sufficient to obtain distinctly different degrees of brightness when they thus appear

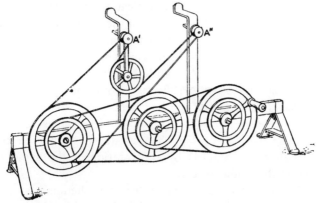

FIG. 26. In the colour wheel here illustrated, the paper discs may be mounted both at A' and at A'',—an arrangement which allows of the simultaneous exhibition and matching of two colour mixtures. In the more usual, simpler form of the colour wheel, the papers can be mounted on one axis only.

to be situated in the same plane, the observer removes the tube and compares the brightness of the papers in ordinary vision.

Three spectral colours are to be chosen, so that when mixed in appropriate proportions on the colour wheel, they give rise to a colourless sensation.

The various hues, spectral and extra-spectral, obtained by mixing these colours in other proportions should be also noted.

(*b*) *Colour mixtures.* The observer finds the complementary colour to any colour, so that the two coloured papers, when turned simultaneously upon the same colour wheel, may give rise to a colourless sensation.

N.B.—It is at first puzzling to find that the blue and yellow papers, placed together on the colour wheel, produce a sensation different from that obtained by mixing blue and yellow pigments; but the explanation is easy. The papers are specially selected for their purity of colour, while ordinary blue and yellow pigments contain green, which becomes evident when the blue and yellow neutralise one another.

Two small coloured paper squares of like dimensions are placed upon a black velvet ground. Between them is set

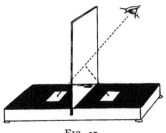

FIG. 27.

a vertical piece of glass; and the head of the observer is so placed that the one colour, seen by light transmitted through the glass, and the other, seen by light reflected from the glass, fall on the same area of the retina (fig. 27). The colour sensation thus produced should be compared with that obtained by the rotation of the same two colours on the colour wheel.

(*c*) *Flicker.* The observer notes the phenomena which attend the gradual extinction of flicker, as a white sector on a black ground is rotated with increasing speed upon the colour wheel. He should look for Charpentier's bands, Fechner's colours (apparent with bright illumination), the coarse flicker, the glitter, the fine flicker, and the finally complete fusion of sensations.

A card of black and white sectors, arranged as in fig. 28 to illustrate the Talbot-Plateau Law, is rotated on the colour wheel. The various rings will be found to assume the same grey.

(*d*) *Brightness estimation.* The brightness of a colour is to be measured by finding a grey background on which it becomes invisible when seen by the peripheral retina. For this purpose the subject fixes his eye on a spot marked upon a large black surface. The experimenter introduces a coloured disc (best mounted on an iron rod), moving it along the black surface until it is seen by the subject as a colourless field. Then various shades of grey are presented at this point along with the colour stimulus, until a grey is found the brightness of which appears to be uniform with that of the colour.

This determination is to be compared with the estimation of brightness obtained by direct comparison. The student should consider what relative effects the Purkinje phenomenon would produce in the two methods.

A semicircle of grey, and one of a colour the brightness of

FIG. 28.

which is to be tested, are arranged so that they form a circular vertical field. A disc composed of alternate open and closed sectors (fig. 29) is then rotated by means of a motor before this field. The observer notes whether flicker is abolished in the coloured or colourless halves of the field at the same moment. He replaces the grey by other shades of grey until flicker disappears in both halves of the circle simultaneously. Once again he compares his results with the two previous methods.

(e) *Simultaneous and successive induction.* A black square on a white background is carefully fixated by the aid of a central white dot. The black becomes brighter, the white darker: ultimately both merge into a uniform grey (the 'simultaneous induction' of Hering). The observer repeats this experiment, using colourless and coloured squares on colourless backgrounds of different brightness. He notes the effects in the after-image (the 'successive induction' of Hering).

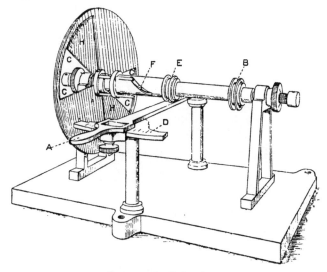

Fig. 29. An Episcotister.

The width of the two open sectors *C C*, *C C*, can be varied by adjusting the sliding graduated plates *H*, *H*. These plates are moved by the arm *A*, which is movable along the graduated scale *D*. The action of the arm *A* is to slide the rim *E*, and the outer tube of which it forms part, round the projecting screw *F*. The sectors are rotated by a reliable motor, a belt from which passes over *B*.

Experiment 38.

Auditory Sensations.

(*a*) *Sound conduction.* The foot of a vibrating tuning-fork *c'*, is applied to the vertex of the head or to the teeth[1]. The tone reaches the ears by bone conduction. It is only when

---

[1] The student should make it a rule to touch the prongs of tuning-forks with the uncovered hand as rarely as possible. The warmth of the hand produces a diminution in pitch, and its moisture makes the forks very liable to rust.

the membranes and ossicles of the middle ear are defective that a fork (of moderate pitch) is audible by bone conduction, when it is inaudible *viâ* the outer and middle ear. This should be verified by observing that after the tone of a fork, applied to the bone behind the ear (the mastoid process), has apparently ceased, the fork can again be heard if it be at once removed and held near the outer ear.

A vibrating tuning-fork is held opposite one ear, at a distance from it exceeding the distance from one ear to the other. When the tone has become too feeble to be audible, the fork is quickly brought close to the ear. It will of course be heard again. A finger is now *lightly* introduced into the opposite ear hole. The effects upon the tone that are produced by alternately withdrawing and reintroducing the finger, should be then observed, and discussed.

(*b*) *Resonance.* The student should familiarise himself with the phenomena of resonance, by using a series of tuning-forks and resonators. He should identify the resonator which is attuned to vibrate to any particular fork. Having by means of a movable clamp, slightly mistuned a fork, he should note the corresponding alterations in reinforcement by the resonator.

If the loud pedal of a pianoforte be pressed down (in order that the strings may be free to vibrate) the resonant effect of singing tones before it may be readily observed.

The external meatus itself behaves as a resonator. One tone more than any other in the neighbourhood of f^{iv} will be found to have a piercing character. The pitch of this tone should be determined by means of a small whistle. The resonant effect of the meatus, thus discovered, may be changed by inserting a piece of rubber tubing about half an inch long into each ear.

(*c*) *Noise.* As opportunity arises, the student should examine the character of different noises introspectively, noting their varying dissimilarity from tones, and endeavouring to detect their pitch. He should depress a great number of adjacent keys on the pianoforte simultaneously,—or still better, sound numerous adjacent tones on a *Tonmesser* (fig. 30), —and observe the noisy character of the resulting experience.

This instrument, once made by the firm of Appunn, and often called after the original maker, contains a series of small metal tongues M which are enclosed in a case and blown by a bellows. The tongues are so attuned that the several tones they emit differ only slightly (by one, two, or four vibrations) from one another. Each tongue can be sounded or silenced by pulling out or pushing in the stop S attached to it. When in use,

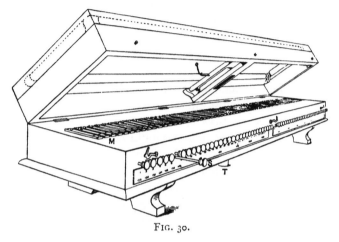

Fig. 30.

the case is closed and mounted on a table containing the bellows, from which air enters the case at T.

The student should notice the effects of coughing or 'clearing the throat' before a pianoforte. The effect of practice upon the detection of pitch in noises is well shown by successively dropping wooden pencils of different lengths on to a wooden table.

Experiment 39.

ON AUDITORY SENSATIONS (*continued*).

(*a*) *Timbre.* Tones of identical pitch should be produced from various instruments (strings, whistles, forks, metal tongues, sirens, etc.) in order that the inherent differences of timbre may be closely noticed. It is easy for the student to analyse the overtones by using the appropriate resonators.

The pitch of the fundamental tone being known, he should calculate the pitch of the harmonic series of its overtones.

The experimenter plucks the string of a monochord, and as its tone is dying away he touches it lightly with a small brush or feather at either of the points which trisect its length. He repeats this several times, the subject always listening carefully to the pitch of the tone produced by the brush. The experimenter touches the string with the brush each time more lightly than before. Ultimately, when the brush is not used at all and the vibrations of the string are allowed to die away undisturbed, the subject will distinctly recognise that overtone of the string, which has the same pitch as the tone produced by the brush. A similar procedure should be adopted in order to detect other overtones of the string.

N.B.—No special musical ability or previous training is required to observe many of these overtones successfully. After a little practice they may be detected in a prolonged note of the pianoforte. An attempt should be made to determine by introspection the effect of such analyses upon the character of the whole tonal experience.

(*b*) *Tone character.* The student should note the characters of pure tones of different pitch.

A fork and its octave fork, mounted on their respective resonance boxes, are simultaneously sounded. As the vibrations lessen the student notes the difference in vowel character produced by stopping the vibrations of the higher fork.

(*c*) *Relations of tones.* The student should familiarise himself on the pianoforte with various intervals within and beyond the octave, playing the tones of each interval both successively and simultaneously, and using the same tonic (Part I, p. 27) throughout. He should note the intimate relation of a tone to its octave, and the differences between the various consonant and dissonant intervals.

The different degrees in which fusion is manifested may be easily studied if the experimenter sound sometimes two tones, and at other times only a single tone, the subject deciding whether one or two tones are present. The number of correct answers given by an unmusical subject varies with the degree of fusion. The ease of analysis of a given interval may be also examined when the latter is increased by one or more octaves.

(*d*) *Intensity of simultaneous tones.* A high fork and a low fork are simultaneously sounded upon their resonance cases, and their vibrations are allowed to die away until the high fork can no longer be heard. If now the vibrations of the low fork be stopped, the high fork will at once be heard again. On the other hand, if the sounds are allowed to continue until the low fork is no longer heard, the audibility of the latter will not be revived by stopping the higher fork. That is to say, a low tone will obliterate a weak high tone far more completely than a high tone will obliterate a weak low tone.

Experiment 40.

On Auditory Sensations (*continued*).

(*a*) *Upper limit of pitch.* The upper limit of hearing is here determined by means of a Galton's whistle.

In blowing the instrument, care must be taken that the wind pressure employed be, as nearly as possible, uniform. The subject sits sideways at about a metre's distance from the experimenter. The latter takes the whistle and sets it so as to produce a relatively low tone. The whistle length is gradually shortened after each note is produced, until a point is reached when the subject can hear no tone, but only the puff of the windblast. The experimenter records the length of the whistle at this point, shortens it yet a little, and then commences a fresh series of observations, gradually lengthening the whistle until the subject just recognises the presence of a tone. Again the experimenter records the whistle length. Five pairs of such records should be taken, and the mean of the ten estimations be determined.

(*b*) *Binaural differences in pitch.* The subject holds two tuning-forks of identical pitch, one in each hand, ready for the experimenter to strike them. The subject then lifts them several times alternately, the right-hand fork to the right ear, the left-hand fork to the left ear, and will perhaps ultimately decide that the two forks appear to be of different pitch. The experimenter applies a light clamp or a small lump of wax to the prongs of the apparently higher-sounding fork, and hands them to the observer. They are struck by the experimenter, and the observer again compares their tones. The clamp is raised or lowered until the tones appear identical.

N.B.—In seeking to account for the differences (if any) obtained, the student must bear in mind the various circumstances (Part I, pp. 29, 30) in which an illusory change of pitch is possible.

(*c*) *Beats and their character.* The student simultaneously sounds the two forks, which have been brought to apparently identical pitch in the previous experiment. He proceeds to count the beats, aided, if necessary, by holding the two forks over a single resonator. Provided that the frequency of the beats do not exceed five per second, they may be counted directly. Beyond this limit, an intermediate fork must be introduced, which is to be sounded first with one and then with the other fork, the beats being counted in each case. The beats are to be

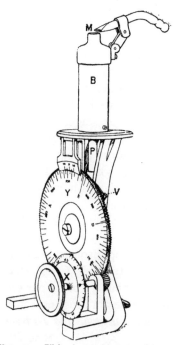

Fig. 31.—This instrument consists essentially of a bottle *B* which is blown at its mouth *M*. The column of air within the bottle is shortened or lengthened by the upward or downward movement of the piston *P*. The piston is moved by the rotation of a peculiarly shaped metal disc, the edge of which is just visible at *V*. The rotation of this disc (or 'variator') is dependent on movement of the two connected graduated wheels *Y* and *X*, the latter of which, when manipulated by the experimenter, thus effects minute or relatively gross changes in the pitch of the note emitted by the bottle.

counted singly, or in pairs or in fours. Ten counts in all should be made, by different methods of reckoning, if possible. The counting must be begun when the position of the hand of the watch, as it lies exactly over a second's mark, coincides with a beat. The student must start thus: 0, 1, 2, 3, 4; he must remember to deduct one from the result if he start from unity. He should count for fifteen seconds, and then calculate the mean number of beats counted per second. Then he can express in terms of a fraction of a tone the difference between the two ears in the determinations of pitch.

The four stages, alluded to in Part I, pp. 36, 37, should be observed as the frequency of beats is slowly increased. Two tuning forks giving c' may be employed, the pitch of one of which is gradually lowered by adjustable clamps. Stern's Tone Variators, however (fig. 31) provide a far more convenient apparatus.

Beats obtained from different tone regions are to be compared.

A comparison is made, if possible, between the successive pairs of tones C_0 G_0, G_0 c°, c° e°, e° g°, c' d', b' c'', each of which gives about 33 beats per second. The student should note the differences in roughness according to the tone region.

(*d*) *Intertone and Difference Tone.* The pitch of the beating

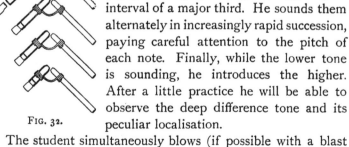

tone (the intertone) is carefully noted as the interval between two nearly identical tones is increased.

The student takes two Quincke's tubes (fig. 32) of high pitch, *e.g.* c^{iv}, e^{iv}, giving an interval of a major third. He sounds them alternately in increasingly rapid succession, paying careful attention to the pitch of each note. Finally, while the lower tone is sounding, he introduces the higher. After a little practice he will be able to observe the deep difference tone and its peculiar localisation.

FIG. 32.

The student simultaneously blows (if possible with a blast of regulated constant pressure) two ordinary piston whistles,—

better still, two of Stern's Tone Variators (fig. 31),—starting from unison and gradually raising the pitch of one of them. At first only beats are heard; next, possibly the difference tone of the second order; later, the very low difference tone of the first order appears, which rises in pitch as the interval between the primary tones increases.

The student takes two tuning-forks of known pitch, which give an audible difference tone of the first order. He sounds these on their resonance boxes and compares the pitch of the difference tone with that of a suitable simultaneously sounding fork, the tone of which can be varied by means of an adjustable clamp. Beats will be heard as the pitch of the latter fork is brought near to that of the difference tone, the beats becoming slower with diminishing difference of pitch and disappearing when absolute unison is reached. In order to determine the pitch of the difference tone, the pitch of the tone given by the fork thus clamped must be found by making it beat with another fork of known pitch.

If two Quincke's tubes (with corks removed) which lie a major seventh apart (8 : 15) be sounded together, careful observation will reveal the presence of the deep difference tone of the second order lying three octaves below the lower tone.

(*e*) *Least perceptible difference of pitch.* Probably tuning-forks will be the most convenient instruments for the student's use. No source of sound, however, is entirely free from disadvantages; there is varying difficulty in securing uniformity of loudness, pitch and timbre. The method of serial groups (Part I, p. 196) may be recommended for the elementary student.

The influence of time order (standard presented first or second) should be studied. Full introspective records should be obtained from the subject, with regard to imagery, tendencies to movement of the glottis, and his modes of arriving at a judgment.

Experiment 41.

OLFACTORY ACUITY.

The experimenter dissolves a gram of camphor in 1000 c.c. of odourless distilled or rain water. He prepares from this a series of camphor solutions, of strengths 1 : 4000, 1 : 8000, 1 : 16,000, 1 : 32,000, etc. A number of cylindrical glass tubes, closed at one end, must be in readiness. They should measure about 75 mm. in height and 25 mm. in width, and be scrupulously clean and free from smell.

The experimenter first attempts to arrive at an extremely rough determination of the olfactory acuity of the subject, by asking him to smell the variously diluted camphor solutions successively. Only one or two minutes should be given to this part of the experiment, in order to avoid the onset of fatigue. The solutions are, therefore, rapidly sniffed in succession, until a solution is reached in which no odour of camphor can be detected.

The experimenter begins with a camphor solution which is a stage stronger than that which appears to be roughly liminal. While the subject is resting (in order that he may recover as completely as possible from the just-mentioned procedure), the experimenter takes four of the cylindrical glass vessels, two of which are to contain 50 c.c. of odourless water, and two the same amount of the solution of camphor. The vessels are marked, preferably on their base, so that the contents of each are identifiable only by the experimenter. He now prepares a scheme of five different orders in which the four vessels are to be successively presented to the subject. It is well to prepare two such schemes, and to use sometimes one, and sometimes the other, so that the subject cannot possibly become acquainted with the orders.

An interval of fifteen minutes having elapsed, the four tubes are now set before the subject, who bends over and smells them successively. He is not allowed to touch them, or to return to a solution after he has given a reply. He is to answer 'Camphor' or 'Water,' before he proceeds from one solution to smell the next. The subject then turns his back, while the experimenter changes the order of the same four vessels, in accordance with his scheme. The subject smells them again. The order is then changed, and they are smelled again, the procedure being repeated until the twenty replies are recorded. Record is carefully kept of all answers, and an arbitrary threshold is fixed which allows two wrong answers in ten in respect of the camphor solutions.

If, as is probable, the limit has not been reached, the experiments are continued by substituting a weaker solution of camphor in the next series.

A pause of ten minutes should be allowed in passing from one series of twenty answers to the next.

Occasionally a fifth vessel containing either camphor solution or water, or instead of four, only three vessels may be exposed, in order to avoid certain inferences on the part of the subject; but the cautions mentioned in Part I, p. 196 must be borne in mind.

The experimenter should gradually pass to a solution the strength of which is definitely below that required for the arbitrary threshold. He should then reverse the previous procedure and present increasing strengths of the solution until the threshold is once again reached and overstepped.

Experiment 42.

Sensory Adaptation.

(*a*) The observer should investigate the effects of wearing coloured glasses for some time.

(*b*) *Purkinje's Images.* The experimenter and the subject are in a dark room. The former concentrates the light of a candle by means of a double convex lens of short focus on to the outer (temporal) corner of the subject's sclerotic, who turns his eye inwards, regarding preferably a light-coloured patternless wall. The subject will soon see the shadows of the retinal vessels as a dark arborescence on a yellowish-red field. Under ordinary conditions these vessels are invisible, mainly owing to sensory adaptation.

(*c*) *The blind spot.* The existence of the blind spot, the point of entrance of the optic nerve, may be conveniently demonstrated here, although the filling out of this spot (which occurs under the ordinary conditions of daily life) is not exactly an instance of adaptation. Although the spot is devoid of rods and cones, the subject irresistibly supplies the sensations which are actually wanting there, being guided by the mode in which neighbouring sensitive regions of the retina

✱

FIG. 33.

are being simultaneously stimulated. A simple method of demonstrating the blind spot consists in closing one eye (the left) while the other is fixed on a point marked on a card (fig. 33). At some distance to one side of the point the card bears a circle, which disappears when the card is moved to such a distance from the eye that while the image of the point falls on the fovea, that of the circle falls on the blind spot.

(*d*) *Auditory adaptation.* The subject places the ends of a rubber tube one in each ear, and sits before a table on which the tube rests. The experimenter gently rests a vibrating tuning-fork on the midpoint of the tube, compressing the latter to one side so that the tone is conducted only to one ear. As soon as it ceases to be audible to the subject, the observer gently releases the tube on the other side of the fork, so that the hitherto unused path is now available.

The subject places a vibrating fork on the vertex of his head and retains it until the tone appears to have died away. Then he removes it only for an instant and places it as before on the head.

If in these two experiments the tone is again heard after it had disappeared, the student should consider the various factors on which the phenomenon may depend.

Experiment 43.

TACTUAL LOCALISATION.

(*a*) The experimenter takes the compass, the points of which are set at a distance 2 cm. apart, and draws it with uniform movement and pressure across the cheek of the subject from ear to lip. The subject observes the changes in apparent distance between the points and in their apparent rate of movement.

(*b*) *Aristotle's experiment.* The subject places his hand palm upwards on the table, and the experimenter crosses the subject's ring finger over the middle finger. The experiment consists in simultaneously touching the adjacent sides of the tips of the crossed fingers with a single object. This is done by the experimenter, the subject being blindfolded and ignorant whether he will be touched by one or by two objects.

Several modifications of the experiment have been described. Instead of touching the ulnar side of the middle and the radial side of the ring finger, as above, two touches may be simultaneously applied, one to the radial side of the middle finger, the other to the ulnar side of the ring finger. Or the distances may be compared when two compass points are simultaneously applied one to each of the crossed fingers, the points first being close together, and secondly much wider apart. Or again, the compass points may be applied diagonally (instead of, as in the previous experiment, transversely) across the two finger tips, and the subject be asked in which direction the diagonal lies. Greater pressure may be made on one of the two points, the subject being asked to state which finger is being pressed upon.

The results differ for different individuals, some of the illusions being present in certain people which are not obtainable in others.

Another striking variation of the experiment is as follows. Holding the compass points so that the line joining them is vertical, the experimenter applies them, one to the upper, one to the lower lip of the subject—(i) when the lips are in the normal position, (ii) when they are laterally displaced from each other. The subject estimates the inclination of the imaginary line between the compass points.

(c) *Absolute localisation*. The experimenter makes a 'life size' outline sketch of the subject's left forearm or hand, as it rests comfortably upon a table. He draws in such veins, tendons or skin folds as may serve as landmarks. The subject is blindfolded. His right hand hangs by his side, holding a blunt-pointed wooden rod. After a warning signal, the experimenter touches the subject's left forearm or hand with a similar rod. He removes it after two seconds, whereupon the subject, still blindfold, brings his own rod as precisely as possible to the same spot. The experimenter carefully measures the distance between the two touches, and records the position of each in the diagram, joining the two by a line which bears an arrow indicating the direction of the error, while the length of the line indicates the extent of the error of localisation.

Several such tests are made on various parts of the subject's forearm or hand, the experimenter taking care that the conditions (*e.g.* the duration of his touch, the amount of pressure exerted by it, and the interval between the two touches) remain as constant as possible. The order of the successive tests should be noted on the diagram, and at the end of the series the records should be investigated with the object of showing any general tendency of error, and the influence of practice and of the position of the touch. The experimenter must always be on the look out for anything in the behaviour of the subject, which may throw light on the attitude of the subject during localisation. The latter makes careful introspective observations throughout the experiment, with the same object of revealing the psychological factors involved in his acts of localisation.

The influence of a comparison of the two touches by the subject may be eliminated, by forbidding him to move his rod after he has once touched his skin; or by touching his skin through a hole in a cardboard screen held over the forearm or hand, the screen receiving and recording the subject's attempt at localisation. The factor of knowledge of the position of the limb touched may be eliminated and the influence of visual experience may be heightened by requiring the subject to open his eyes and apply a pencil to a plaster cast, to a photograph of his arm, or to an assistant's forearm or hand placed conveniently before the subject. Visual experience may be studied entirely apart from tactual experience, if a long-previously marked spot on his arm be shown to the subject, who thereupon closes his eyes and endeavours to touch it without subsequent groping. The combined influence of vision and touch may be further investigated by allowing the subject to see the experimenter's touch before he closes his eyes and attempts to localise it. The influence of position and movement on localisation may be investigated by the experimenter moving the subject's limb without allowing him to open his eyes, and then resuming the experiment.

The influence of visual factors on tactual localisation is so great as to increase the accuracy of the act considerably. It is often shown in the tendency of the subject to displace the touch towards serviceable visual landmarks, *e.g.* bony prominences, the margins of the arm, the flexion folds of the skin.

In another method a screen of glass or cardboard, ruled in squares, is held in such a position that one side of it is touched by a finger of one hand of the blindfold subject, who is instructed then to bring the corresponding finger of his other hand to touch the other side of the screen so as to indicate the position of the already placed finger.

Experiment 44.

Binocular Experience.

(*a*) *The Cyclopean Eye.* A piece of paper is held horizontally before the eyes, on which two parallel lines have been drawn, separated by a distance equal to that between pairs of corresponding points. When the gaze, travelling over the two lines along the surface of the paper, is directed to a distant point, only a single line will be seen, situated midway between the two eyes.

(*b*) *Failure to identify eye stimulated.* The experimenter takes a large sheet of black cardboard, pierced with a minute aperture, and he moves the card continuously but irregularly in front of the observer's face, so that light is admitted through the aperture, now to one, now to the other eye. The observer will note that, after these movements have been carried on for a brief time, he is unable to tell which eye is receiving light when the experimenter ceases to move the card.

(*c*) *Rivalry, combination, lustre, contrast.* The effects of binocular colour rivalry, combination and lustre should be studied in one or other form of stereoscope; coloured squares, black and white squares, and various designs and objects being used. The relation of rivalry to discrepancy in contour, intensity or brightness should be observed.

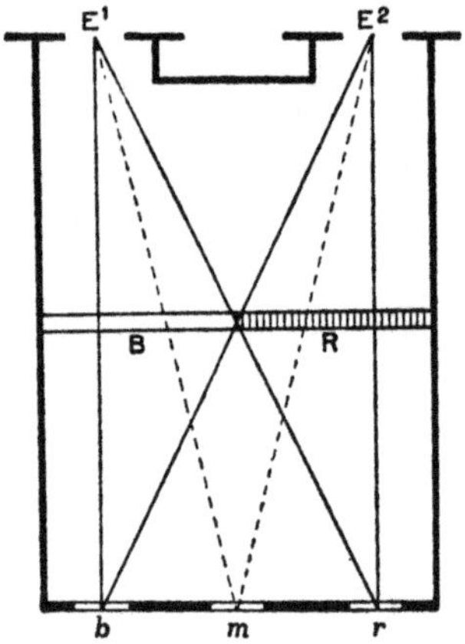

FIG. 34.

Hering has devised an arrangement for showing binocular colour combination and rivalry, in which the two eyes look each through a differently coloured (*e.g.* a blue and a red) glass at a square of white light.

Figure 34 shows this arrangement. *B* and *R* are the blue and red glasses, fixed with their edges juxtaposed in the dark box, to one end of which the eyes, E^1 and E^2, are applied. At the other end are three squares of ground glass, *b*, *m*, and *r*, through which the observer gazes on to a uniform white surface, *e.g.* a clouded sky.

Under these conditions, the two lateral squares are coloured according to the glass placed before the eye, while the central one shows alternating colour combination and rivalry.

By fixating a nearer point, the student produces double images of a white stripe on a black background. He places a red glass before the one eye and an equally bright grey glass before the other. He observes if the image seen through the grey glass is tinged with green (the complementary colour to red). He then removes the red glass and observes that the image, yielded by the eye which has been covered with the grey glass, becomes a well-marked red.

The light of a window is allowed to fall laterally on one eye, while the other is consequently more shaded. The student now doubles the image of a white stripe on a black background by fixating a nearer point. He observes the difference in brightness and colour of the two images.

This experiment is called Fechner's side-window experiment, and is dependent on the exposure of one eye to a brighter light which enters the eye through the sclerotic and iris, acquiring a reddish tinge owing to its passage through a layer of blood vessels. Retinal adaptation and binocular contrast afford a partial explanation of the effects.

The effects of uniocular contrast and binocular combination are observed in a simple apparatus devised by Hering, in which a black stripe on a white ground is doubled by fixation of a nearer point, and is viewed by one eye through a red, by the other through a blue glass.

(d) *Brightness.* The observer places a moderately dark grey glass before one eye which is closed, while the other regards a white surface. He observes the brightness of the latter, and he compares it with its brightness when the shaded eye is opened and the surface is regarded binocularly.

(e) *Listing's Law.* This law may be verified by projecting the after-image of a rectangular cross on to various points on a plane surface. Fig. 35 represents a conveniently prepared surface, the centre of which is occupied by a coloured cross. The head of the subject is comfortably fixed so that it cannot move when the eyes are turned. The subject is seated so that his eyes, when regarding the cross, are in an approximately primary position. This position the subject finds by fixating the cross and by then turning the eyes to one or other of the points *a*, *b*, *c*, *d*. If the outline of the various after-images takes the direction of the horizontal and vertical ruled lines of the surface, the primary position of the eyes has been found. If the surface can be suitably rotated round its centre, the corresponding condition will be found to hold good for oblique as for horizontal and vertical positions of the arms of the cross.

Let the eyes be obliquely turned so as to project the after-images of the vertical and horizontal arms of the cross on to the points *e, f, g* or *h*. The unequal displacements, which the arms of the after-images undergo, are shown by the drawings of the cross at these points in figure. But were the surface of projection a large hemisphere corresponding to the curved surface of the retina, instead of being a plane, these distortions would not occur, and thus Listing's law would be verified. The distortions with which we meet are due to our interpretation of the ruled lines as being truly horizontal and vertical in spite of the fact that the eyes are now regarding them in an oblique instead of in the primary position. Save in the primary position of the eyes, horizontal and vertical lines must really give rise to oblique retinal images. But since these lines are interpreted as being free from obliquity, a corresponding obliquity is transferred to the actually horizontal and vertical bars constituting the after-image of the cross.

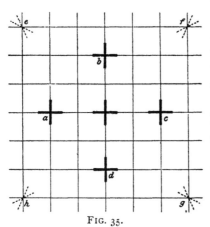

FIG. 35.

Experiment 45.

OPTICAL ILLUSIONS.

A subject and experimenter, after they have familiarised themselves with the commoner forms of geometric optical

illusions, should proceed to the quantitative estimation of one
of them after the following model.

The apparatus may consist of a board covered with black
cloth, on the surface of which appear two white lines at right
angles to one another. By a simple contrivance at the back
of the board, the lengths of these lines may be easily varied.
The experimenter sets the horizontal line at 100 mm. and the
vertical line at a few mm. in length, and gives the board to
the subject, who has to prolong the vertical line until it
appears equal in length to the horizontal line. While he is
lengthening the vertical, the subject must be careful that the
board is in a constant horizontal (or vertical) position directly
below (or in front of) him. By means of compasses, or by
applying a scale to the board, the experimenter notes and
records the actual length of this vertical line. He then
reduces the vertical to a few mm. in length and asks the
subject to repeat the estimation. Ten such values should be
obtained, and their mean and mean variation determined.

Ten estimations should then be made by the subject, when
the vertical is initially longer than the horizontal and has to
be shortened by the subject until the two lines appear equal
in length.

The mean error and variability for the twenty estimations
can then be calculated, and a comparison can be made of the
error and variability of estimation when the vertical is presented to the subject (i) longer and (ii) shorter than the
horizontal line.

By turning the board successively through 90°, 180°, and
270°, three further series of observations should be made in
order to compare the various errors of estimation, according
as the vertical lies to the right of, to the left of, or above or
below the horizontal line.

Experiments may also be conducted, in which the vertical
line preserves a constant length of 100 mm., and the horizontal
has to be made equal to it by the subject.

A very simple apparatus may be also contrived for
measuring the Müller-Lyer illusion; the two parts of the
illusion being combined as shown in the upper portion of

figure 17 in Part I (p. 288). The right-hand half of the figure, with both pairs of end lines, is drawn on a thin white xylonite surface. This part of the apparatus is fixed and forms a framework, to the left of which a thin board of the same material slides in and out, bearing the remainder of the figure. The board can be drawn out or pushed in beneath the framework, until the two sections of the horizontal line appear equal.

Experiment 46.

ESTIMATION OF TIME INTERVALS

(*a*) Refer back to Section 2, Experiment 11 (2) and carry out in full all the tests indicated.

(*b*) *Comparison of filled and unfilled intervals.* A series of experiments should be devised and carried out to show the effect on time estimation which occurs when the interval between the two taps, *a*, *b*, is filled with other taps, instead of being silent. Two intervals are successively presented, the one filled, the other empty, and the subject has to determine whether the intervals are equal or unequal. The time order of presentation of the intervals should be varied, and either the limiting or the constant method should be used to determine the amount of the illusion.

Experiment 47.

RHYTHM.

(*a*) *Subjective accentuation.* The metronome is a convenient instrument for observing the subjective accentuation of the simplest rhythm. But care must be taken that no objective accentuation of its beats exists.

The experimenter should set the metronome at various rates of oscillation, so that the subject may appreciate the relation between rate of rhythm and ease of subjective accentuation. The subject should observe and record the varying affective values (pleasant, wearisome, etc.) of different rhythms and the associated experiences which they may

revive. The experimenter may notice unconscious movements on the part of the subject.

(*b*) *Objective accentuation.* The effects of varying the objective accentuation are easily studied by enclosing the
metronome in a box, the lid of which may be silently opened
and closed at any moment so as to allow any desired sound
to be intensified and so to be accented. Trochaic– ⏑, iambic
⏑ –, dactylic – ⏑ ⏑, anapæstic ⏑ ⏑ –, and cretic – ⏑ – measures
should be studied. The effect of accenting the first of every
four, five and six beats should be studied for different rates
of rhythm.

(*c*) *Reproduction of rhythm.* The accuracy with which the
reproduction of a given rate of rhythm can be maintained
may be investigated by means of the metronome; the subject
reproducing the rhythm by tapping on a Morse key, the
movements of which are transmitted to the recording surface
of a drum in another room. The subject begins to tap syn-
chronously with the metronome sounds, and after, say, twenty
sounds have been heard, the metronome is stopped while the
subject continues his tapping. The time signal or clock (fig. 2)
records fifths of seconds on the drum below the tracings made
by the taps of the subject.

The relation of respiratory movements to rhythmical action
and to the estimation of time may be studied by attaching
a pneumograph (fig. 37) to the subject and by connecting it
with a tambour (fig. 38) brought to bear on the recording
surface.

Experiment 48.

The Memory Image.

It is assumed that the subject has already familiarised himself with the general nature of memory images, by attempting
to revive recent or familiar pictures, scenes or actions. He
now rests his eye on a uniform black screen. After a minute
the experimenter, opening a window in the screen (or by other
means), suddenly exposes for about ten seconds a light or
dark grey disc upon a background of medium greyness.

When this exposure is ended, and the window has been closed, the subject continues dreamily to rest his eyes on the black screen, and he notes whether there is a single or repeated spontaneous revival (perseveration) of the memory after-image, whether the image can be reproduced volitionally, or whether no visual image, worthy of the name, is representable. Preliminary practice is often necessary for the subject to obtain good results. His success will be more assured if the screen be provided with blackened side wings, so that no external objects distract his gaze. Care must be taken not to confuse the sensory with the memory after-image (Part I, p. 140).

The experiment may be modified by similarly exposing a second grey disc, somewhat lighter or darker than the first, the two exposures being separated by an interval of half a minute. The subject endeavours, when the second exposure is over, to compare the two greys, observing to what extent he makes use of the memory image of each.

In a quiet, preferably darkened, room the subject listens for about twenty seconds to a tone uniformly and continuously sounding from some form of whistle. After the tone has ceased, he observes the memory image.

N.B.—In these experiments the subject should notice that the memory image only appears and can only be held fast for a brief time. Its characters should be compared with those of the original presentation. He should observe the feeling of tension in the head and any changes in the localisation of this feeling, during the exposure of the disc and during the appearance of the memory image. The effects of momentary and prolonged exposures should be compared.

Experiment 49.

Muscular Practice.

It is not difficult to devise experiments which shall test the degree of practice in speed and accuracy of movement. Learning how to typewrite, and aiming successive balls at the centre of a target, are examples. The target may be covered with two sheets of paper, between which is inserted a piece of carbon paper. By such means the effects of increasing practice, fatigue, and the extent of retention of practice can be quantitatively determined.

Experiment 50.

FLUCTUATIONS OF ATTENTION.

The subject is seated in a silent room or gallery—or, better still, out of doors on a quiet night. The experimenter holds a watch opposite one ear of the subject, and keeping it at this level, withdraws it in a straight line from the subject, until the latter can only just hear the ticks. The watch may be hidden in a cloth if it tick too loudly. Care must be taken

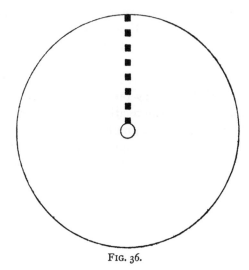

FIG. 36.

that the alternations of sound and silence, now experienced by the subject, are not complicated by any objective variations in the loudness of the ticks. The alternations may be graphically recorded, as in the following experiment.

When a white disc, bearing a thick broken black line on an imaginary radius (fig. 36), is rotated on the colour wheel, a series of grey bands are observed which become increasingly faint towards the periphery of the disc. The subject, comfortably seated, with his head supported by a head rest, fixates the faintest grey ring he can distinguish. He observes the fluctuations that it undergoes.

After a little practice, he will find no difficulty in recording these fluctuations, by varying the pressure of his finger on a rubber bulb which is connected with a recording tambour (fig. 38). The lever of this tambour and a time marker are brought to bear on the travelling smoked surface of a drum or kymograph. The recording instruments should be placed at some distance from the subject, to prevent distraction. The kymograph should rotate quite slowly, say twice in three minutes. The record should be interrupted after a single revolution of the kymograph; a longer sitting becomes unsatisfactory, owing to inattention.

The experiment may be modified in various ways. Instead of a rubber bulb, which permits of a continuous record, a reaction key may be used. Instead of the faintest ring, a ring somewhat less faint may be fixated. The background, instead of being white, may be black and the line white. The degree of attention given by the subject to the ring may be experimentally varied. The relation of respiratory movements to these fluctuations may be graphically studied.

It is essential that the graphic records obtained by the experimenter be supplemented by careful introspection on the part of the subject.

Experiment 51.

EXPRESSION OF FEELING.

(a) *The pneumograph.* N.B.—The brief description of the few following instruments is only intended to give the student an idea of the general principles on which they are constructed. The details of the instruments are certain to differ in different laboratories. It must be left for the teacher to indicate, and for the student to learn by experience, the exact methods of manipulation. The tracings, made by the instruments on a recording surface, need to be accompanied by two other tracings. Of these the one records time intervals of a second while the other indicates the moments of applying and discontinuing the stimulus which is to cause a change of feeling.

This instrument records the rate and extent of respiratory movements. In the simple form figured (fig. 37), it consists

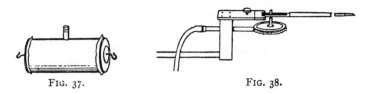

FIG. 37.   FIG. 38.

of a metal cylinder closed at the two ends by rubber sheeting. A hook is attached to the centre of each piece of rubber, the two hooks being connected by a piece of tape which passes tightly round the chest of the subject. The fluctuations of air pressure within the pneumograph, thus produced by respiratory movements, are communicated to a recording tambour (fig. 38) by means of a side opening in the metal wall of the cylinder to which a piece of rubber tubing is attached.

In a complete investigation of respiratory movements, two pneumographs should be employed, since variations in the thoracic movements are by no means always accompanied by like variations in the abdominal movements of respiration.

(*b*) *The sphygmograph.* This sensitive instrument (of which there are very different forms), when applied to the pulse, *e.g.* at the wrist, responds to minute changes in arterial pressure. These changes, constituting the pulse, are communicated by levers to a recording surface. Variations in the form of the pulse curve or in the frequency of the pulse are indicated on the sphygmographic record.

(*c*) *The plethysmograph.* This consists of a closed chamber in which part of the body, usually the forearm, comfortably rests. The chamber is connected with a distant tambour, so that any variations of pressure due to increased or decreased volume of the arm are transmitted to a recording lever. In some patterns of the instrument, the chamber enclosing the arm contains air, but more usually the air is replaced by lukewarm water.

(*d*) *The automatograph.* In investigating the effect of pleasant and unpleasant stimuli upon the contraction of skeletal muscle, it is of course essential that the subject should so far as possible remain in ignorance of the effects which are expected to occur, and that the effects which have occurred should be concealed from him until all the desired experiments are completed.

The automatograph is a convenient instrument for recording involuntary movements of the arm (fig. 39). It is a freely

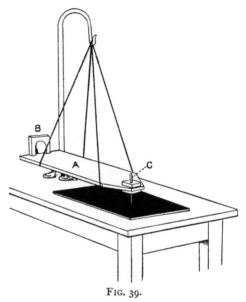

FIG. 39.

swinging 'planchette' *A B*, in which the arm comfortably rests. The slightest to and fro, or lateral, movement of the apparatus is communicated by a glass style *C* to an underlying piece of smoked paper. The subject's eyes are closed throughout the experiment.

The movements of the automatograph should first be studied when the subject preserves a dreamy attitude of complete indifference. After this has been done, the experimenter observes the effect of introducing a pleasant or unpleasant stimulus. Odours (*e.g.* asafœtida, castor oil, musk, jockey club) are the easiest to use; they can be silently brought beneath the subject's nostrils. Their effect on involuntary movement is to be carefully noted by the experimenter and correlated with the introspective record subsequently obtained from the subject.

It is important that a given odour should not be brought into the room until it is needed, and that the subject should be given ample rest between the applications of different stimuli.

(*e*) *The recording dynamometer.* For rough work the instrument figured below (fig. 40) will suffice. Its purpose has been sufficiently indicated in Part I, p. 310. A very

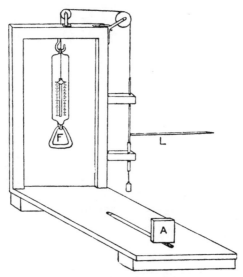

FIG. 40. (After Titchener.)

slowly rotating drum should be used to record the movements of the lever *L*. The subject is enjoined to make a maximal contraction at *F* and to concentrate his attention on maintaining this degree of contraction for about a minute. The eyes are closed as before. A time signal records seconds upon the drum. A preliminary tracing is taken with the subject in an indifferent state. The subject should carefully analyse the state of his consciousness throughout the experiment. After adequate pauses, tracings are taken in which the state of indifference is replaced by one of pleasure or displeasure, owing to the exhibition of an appropriate stimulus at recorded times.

Experiment 52.

STATISTICAL METHODS.

(a) *The Mean, Standard Deviation, Probable Error, etc.*

The student is advised to work out their values for himself from the series of measurements given in the first of the following columns:

v'	d	d^2	v''
190	− 4	16	190
197	+ 3	9	190
196	+ 2	4	191
191	− 3	9	191
195	+ 1	1	192
192	− 2	4	194
194	0	0	195
196	+ 2	4	195
199	+ 5	25	196
190	− 4	16	196
191	− 3	9	196
196	+ 2	4	197
195	+ 1	1	199
13 $\lfloor$ 2522	13 $\lfloor$ 32	13 $\lfloor$ 102	
Av. = 194	*m.v.* 2·46	$\sigma^2 = 7\cdot846$	
		$\sigma = 2\cdot8$ Mdn = 195.	

In the first column the average is determined; in the second, the mean variation ; and in the third, the standard deviation. The fourth column gives the values of v' in numerical order, showing the median at 195 and the quartiles at 191 and 196. Half the difference between the quartiles, namely, 2·5, gives the semi-interquartile range—a third measure of the variability of the series.

No mean is of any value unless it be accompanied by a figure expressing the variability of members of the series. But only one of these three measures of variability need ever be calculated for a given series. The most usual among psychologists is the mean variation. But it is less simple than the semi-interquartile range and less useful than the standard deviation, from which the probable error, E, of the mean may be determined by the formula—

$$E = \frac{0.6745\ \sigma}{\sqrt{n}}.$$

N.B.—When the mean variation is being calculated, it is convenient to arrange the +, zero, and − values of d separately, thus:

+ 3	o	− 4	
+ 2		− 3	The + and − values should
+ 1		− 2	be numerically equal, if the
+ 2		− 4	values of d and the mean have
+ 5		− 3	been correctly determined.
+ 2			
+ 1			
+ 16		− 16	

(*b*) *Correlation.*

The correlation between the following thirteen ($= n$) pairs of measurements, v_x, v_y, is here determined, the means of the two series being 194, 145 and their standard deviation 2·8, 3·4 respectively.

	v_x	v_y	x	y	xy
A	190	140	− 4	− 5	+ 20
B	197	150	+ 3	+ 5	+ 15
C	196	144	+ 2	− 1	− 2
D	191	140	− 3	− 5	+ 15
E	195	144	+ 1	− 1	− 1
F	192	148	− 2	+ 3	− 6
G	194	146	o	+ 1	o
H	196	152	+ 2	+ 7	+ 14
I	199	146	+ 5	+ 1	+ 5
J	190	142	− 4	− 3	+ 12
K	191	143	− 3	− 2	+ 6
L	196	145	+ 2	o	o
M	195	145	+ 1	o	o

$$\Sigma\ (xy) = \quad 78$$

Thus $\dfrac{\Sigma\ (xy)}{n\,\sigma_x \sigma_y} = 0.63$.

By the simpler method (Part I, p. 124) of giving orders of rank to *A, B, C,* etc., we have

	v_x	v_y	d	$(2d)^2$
A	1½	1½	0	0
B	12	12	0	0
C	10	5½	4½	81
D	3½	1½	2	16
E	7½	5½	2	16
F	5	11	6	144
G	6	9½	3½	49
H	10	13	3	36
I	13	9½	3½	49
J	1⅓	3	1½	9
K	3½	4	1½	1
L	10	7½	2½	25
M	7½	7½	0	

$$\Sigma\,(2d)^2 = 426$$

When, as here happens, two or more individuals tie in rank, they are each given a figure intermediate between the ranks which they would occupy if they did not tie. To avoid squaring fractions, $2d$ has been squared instead of d. The fraction in the second of the alternative formulæ quoted on page 124 must therefore be divided by four. It thus runs:

$$r = 1 - \frac{6\Sigma\,(2d)^2}{4n\,(n^2 - 1)}$$

whence

$$r = 0\cdot70.$$

The discrepancy between the results of the two methods is unusually great in this particular case, and is partly due to the large number of tied cases.

N.B.—When the mean and standard deviations have to be calculated for long series, much time and labour may be saved by taking an approximately central variate (obtained merely by casual inspection of the series) and by subtracting each member of the series from this value. Let the algebraical sum of these several differences, divided by the number (n) of individual values, be represented by v_1. Then v_1, when added (with due regard of sign) to the assumed central value, will be found to give the average.

So, too, let the sum of the same differences, severally

squared, be divided by the number of individual values, and let this sum be represented by v_2. Then

$$\sigma = \sqrt{v_2 - v_1{}^2}.$$

Finally, if in two correlated series, $\Sigma\,(x^1 y^1)$ represent the sum of the products of individual pairs of differences from the two central values (chosen as before), and if v_x, v_y, σ_x, σ_y represent the values of v_1 and σ in each series, then the formula for the coefficient of correlation becomes

$$\frac{\Sigma\,(x^1 y^1) - n v_x v_y}{n \sigma_x \sigma_y}.$$

By such means a considerable saving in calculation is reached in determining the mean, the standard deviation, or the coefficient of correlation for lengthy series.

For EU product safety concerns, contact us at Calle de José Abascal, 56–1°,
28003 Madrid, Spain or eugpsr@cambridge.org.

www.ingramcontent.com/pod-product-compliance
Ingram Content Group UK Ltd.
Pitfield, Milton Keynes, MK11 3LW, UK
UKHW012338130625
459647UK00009B/364